T0262458

SPLENDOUR
TENDER

Abi Morgan

# TWO PLAYS

Splendour
Tender

OBERON BOOKS
LONDON

First published in this collection in 2006 by Oberon Books Ltd
521 Caledonian Road, London N7 9RH
Tel: +44 (0) 20 7607 3637 / Fax: +44 (0) 20 7607 3629
e-mail: info@oberonbooks.com
www.oberonbooks.com

*Splendour* first published by Oberon in 2000

*Tender* first published by Oberon in 2001

A catalogue record for this book is available from the British Library.

PB ISBN: 9781840024036
E ISBN: 9781783192274

# Contents

# SPLENDOUR

# Characters

**MICHELEINE**
the wife, female, late 40s

**GILMA**
the interpreter, female, early/mid 20s

**KATHRYN**
the photographer, female, mid/late 30s

**GENEVIEVE**
the informer, female, early/mid 40s

Setting: The play is set in a house, in an affluent neighbourhood on the edge of a large city.

The sound of fireworks/shelling should be abstract.

*Splendour* was first performed by Paines Plough in association with The Peter Wolff Theatre Trust at the Traverse Theatre on 3 August 2000, with the following cast:

MICHELEINE, Mary Cunningham

KATHRYN, Faith Flint

GENEVIEVE, Myra McFadyen

GILMA, Eileen Walsh

Director, Vicky Featherstone

Designer, Neil Warmington

*A woman. MICHELEINE. Late 40s. Sassy. Elegant. A drink somewhere. Always near. GILMA. Mid 20s. Less well dressed. Stooped on the floor sweeping up something with a pan and brush. KATHRYN. Mid/late 30s. More robust. Absorbed in looking at a painting. GENEVIEVE. Early/mid 40s. Dressed as if in a rush. Hair wet, bag in hand, flushed from the outside. Pulling off a scarf as if she has just come from outside.*

MICHELEINE: Genevieve, your hair it's –

GENEVIEVE: Snow.

KATHRYN: ...dripping on her green dress.

GENEVIEVE: I'm fine. The roads are terrible.

(*GILMA sweeps up on the floor.*)

MICHELEINE: It's nothing, just a bit of glass. (*Introducing.*) Gilma.

GENEVIEVE: Gilma.

GILMA: Don't look me up and down like that.

GENEVIEVE: I had to take the back route. Is there anything to drink?

MICHELEINE: Yes. We're onto our third.

(*GENEVIEVE walks across the room and pours herself a glass of vodka.*)

I am sitting in a garden a few hours before this moment. My husband is to my left –

GENEVIEVE: Jesus –

MICHELEINE: ...we are having lunch with friends.

GENEVIEVE: (*I.e. drink.*) ...Micha, where did you get this?

MICHELEINE: Lunch with Isabella.

KATHRYN: We are drinking chilli vodka.

GENEVIEVE: You saw her?

MICHELEINE: A few hours ago.

KATHRYN: It is blindingly hot.

MICHELEINE: To my right is a pudgy man I always seem to get stuck with. He laughs too much at a joke my husband makes –

(*GILMA hands MICHELEINE back the dustpan and brush.*)

GILMA: (*To MICHELEINE.*) I'm sorry.

MICHELEINE: Of course, it's a very funny joke...

GENEVIEVE: I thought Oolio would be –

MICHELEINE: Coming. You know the office. You're
dripping on the carp –

GENEVIEVE: (*To MICHELEINE.*) Micha, there are bells
ringing all along the Southside.

(*A beat. GENEVIEVE clocks KATHRYN looking at the
painting.*)

MICHELEINE: A nun is walking through a park when a
giant gorilla attacks her. He ravishes her in the bushes and
then quickly bounds away. Clearly distressed and returning
to her convent her Mother Superior with some concern
takes the young nun aside. 'My dear I can't help but notice,
you seem very upset of late.'

GENEVIEVE: The painting –

(*GENEVIEVE comes up to look at the painting with
KATHRYN.*)

I see you've noticed the painting.

KATHRYN: Sorry?

GENEVIEVE: The painting? You like it?

MICHELEINE: We commissioned it. It's not one of his best.

KATHRYN: I'm sorry... (*To GILMA.*) Gilma?

(*To GENEVIEVE.*) I'm sorry. I don't understand.

MICHELEINE: (*Introducing.*) Kathryn.

KATHRYN: (*To GENEVIEVE.*) Kathryn.

MICHELEINE: (*To GENEVIEVE.*) She's a very important
journalist.

KATHRYN: I've come to take a photograph.

MICHELEINE: This is my best friend, Genevieve. Our
husbands have been, were friends for twenty –

GENEVIEVE: ...five –

MICHELEINE: ...years.

(*GENEVIEVE and KATHRYN shake hands.*)

KATHRYN: Gilma?

GILMA: The painting. Her husband –

KATHRYN: ...painted it? We're discussing fucking painting.

MICHELEINE: (*To KATHRYN.*) Won't you have a little nut?
Moved by the Mother Superior's vigilante concern, the
young nun confesses to the recent contretemps with the

gorilla in the park. The Mother Superior bestows sympathy but as the weeks pass, a vow of silence is shrouded over the terrible event. But one day the Mother Superior, unable to contain herself, betrays a certain curiosity, a certain girlish interest... 'My dear, don't think me indiscreet, but may I ask did it hurt?' 'Of course it hurt Mother Superior, I mean imagine this big gorilla, he never rings, he never writes, there's not a –'

Midway through the punch line, the pudgy man, who is already laughing, suddenly shoots up and says... 'Ssh, did you hear that?'

GILMA: (*To GENEVIEVE.*) The bells on the Southside. I heard them, this afternoon.

MICHELEINE: 'Faint, on a cold breeze.' (*Beat.*) I heard nothing at all.

GILMA: There were people, they were dancing –

MICHELEINE: No.

GILMA: (*To MICHELEINE.*) And soldiers being paraded.

GENEVIEVE: Micheleine –

GILMA: That is impossible. You must have been –

MICHELEINE: I must have been –

GILMA: ...very far away.

KATHRYN: What did she say?

(*GILMA shakes her head.*)

MICHELEINE: I sat next to that pudgy man –

GENEVIEVE: Who laughs at almost anything?

MICHELEINE: Oolio did his usual –

GENEVIEVE: Not?

MICHELEINE: The gorilla and the nun.

(*MICHELEINE and GENEVIEVE laugh.*)

'Of course it hurt Mother Superior, I mean imagine this big gorilla, he never rings, he never writes, there's not a bunch of flowers in sight...'

And we're laughing but the truth is –

KATHRYN: Why the hell are they laughing?

MICHELEINE: ...I want to but today –

GILMA: (*Touching GENEVIEVE.*) Fuck, you're freezing.

MICHELEINE: ...I don't get the joke at all.

13

KATHRYN: I am standing in the foyer of a large hotel a few
hours before this moment. In a city that is familiar,
a city I have been to several times before. This job that
I have come for, this job is particular. I have been
travelling since five a.m. Greenwich Meantime. I am tired.
At the airport there is no one to meet me. It's the usual.
I pick up a taxi. The taxi is expensive, too expensive, I
argue. I win my case.

MICHELEINE: This portrait of my husband?

GILMA: This portrait that you plan to take? You must be
patient with him. He rarely courts press.

KATHRYN: It was agreed through your office.

GILMA: A request from his advisors. It was a personal
invitation.

MICHELEINE: We're delighted you could come.

GILMA: (*To GENEVIEVE.*) It's snowing.

GENEVIEVE: Only a little now.

GILMA: ...You drove along the...

GENEVIEVE: Past the Gymnasium...

GILMA: ...I use to swim there as a child...

GENEVIEVE: Since they bombed the bridge last August it's
the only route to take.

KATHRYN: I arrive at my hotel. There are large lions and a
plastic flamingo arrangement in the foyer. The man in the
lobby reassures me that they are not real. Reclaimed since
the Zoo was bombed. There is frost on the lion's mane.
(*The phone rings.*)

MICHELEINE: Genie, your hair. I'll get you a towel.
(*MICHELEINE eats. The phone stops ringing.*)

KATHRYN: I ask if there have been any messages for me and
a girl standing in the lobby, a girl wearing a coat that is
clearly not hers, a girl wearing a coat that is weighed down
with shoulder pads, a girl –

GILMA: (*To KATHRYN.*) From newspaper? Excuse me?
You've come to take the photograph?

KATHRYN: ...with an accent I can barely understand –

GILMA: I'm interpreter. The car's... You come? This way.

KATHRYN: (*To GILMA.*) My office?

GILMA: Yes. They contact me.

KATHRYN: They arranged for you to take me?

GILMA: (*To KATHRYN.*) Gilma.

KATHRYN: (*Nodding.*) Gilma. (*Beat.*) She barely understands
me. In my mind I am sticking pins in the office PA.
(*MICHELEINE comes in, dropping a towel in GENEVIEVE's
lap.*)

GENEVIEVE: Micha –

MICHELEINE: Genie, what are we to do with you?

GENEVIEVE: Was that Oolio on the telephone?

MICHELEINE: Yes, he's on his way. Gilma? A Northern
name.

GILMA: Not always.

MICHELEINE: How's Darius?

GENEVIEVE: He called last week. I think there's a new
girlfriend –

MICHELEINE: A girlfriend at last. We had money on it
he was –

GENEVIEVE: And Marcus wrote. He's going to bring Gina
and the children to stay.

MICHELEINE: (*Eyeing KATHRYN.*) She's watching me.
(*Beat.*) That's good. That's lovely, Genie –

GILMA: Stockings –

MICHELEINE: Italian.

GILMA: With underwear I bet to match.

MICHELEINE: Gilma… I wonder I didn't clock that right
away.

GILMA: (*To MICHELEINE.*) Nice glasses.

MICHELEINE: Siberian. (*Beat.*) Thank you.

GILMA: You're welcome.

MICHELEINE: That sounds very American.

GILMA: Sorry?

MICHELEINE: 'You're welcome'? (*Beat.*) That's very
American.

GILMA: The University of California. I studied abroad.
(*KATHRYN holds up her bag to MICHELEINE.*)

KATHRYN: Is it okay, if I…? Gilma?

GILMA: Is it okay? To unpack her things?

MICHELEINE: Please tell her, of course –

GILMA: (*To KATHRYN.*) It's fine.

MICHELEINE: (*Calling out.*) Marianna… Will she need some help?

(*KATHRYN shakes her head.*)

GENEVIEVE: The painting is of the city. That is the river and that is the persons… I speak a little of your language…

KATHRYN: Someone should tell her very badly. (*Beat.*) The persons?

GENEVIEVE: Yes. The persons of the town.

KATHRYN: And which bit are the people?

GENEVIEVE: There are the persons.

KATHRYN: Right.

GENEVIEVE: You see their faces?

KATHRYN: I see. Yes. I see. Right. Is that a cow?

(*The phone rings. And rings.*)

MICHELEINE: (*Calling out.*) Marianna, Marianna, will you please get the telephone?

(*The phone stops ringing.*)

No matter. (*Calling out.*) Marianna. (*To herself.*) We need more ice.

(*MICHELEINE goes out.*)

GENEVIEVE: How did you get here?

GILMA/KATHRYN: Taxi.

GILMA: The office said you'd pay it.

KATHRYN: I know this is a lie. A blatant, shameless lie. The office have included it, she has already been paid once today.

GILMA: If there's going to be a problem –

KATHRYN: I reassure her there's not a problem, but I know the tricks they all readily have –

GILMA: It takes on average –

GENEVIEVE: Twenty minutes, fifteen if you're lucky.

GILMA: It's a forty-minute ride. It's better if we pay him. He won't drive us anywhere until he sees there's cash.

KATHRYN: He takes us on the scenic route. The view is one I'm used to, one we've all come to expect. (*Beat.*) She'll ask

for forty and I'll know it will only cost twenty. She splits
the extra and the driver gets the ride. (*Beat.*) And he will
come back for us? For sure before midnight? The office are
waiting?

She nods. (*Beat.*) I don't trust her.

GILMA: (*Nodding.*) She's mean with her money.

KATHRYN: Her shoulder pads crunch as she climbs in the
car.

GILMA: The driver is a friend, a friend of my brother's. He's
a gambler and a user. I hold back ten. That way he'll come
back. That way she won't criticise. Please do not worry.
The door?

KATHRYN: Huh?

GILMA: Not closed.

KATHRYN: (*Beat.*) She leans across me and there is a faint
smell of BO.

(*MICHELEINE comes through, a bucket of ice in her hand.*)

MICHELEINE: Do you know I went out and found the front
door wide open? We now have ice both inside and out.
(*Holding up ice.*) Genevieve, you said the traffic –

GENEVIEVE: A log-jam all along the North route.

MICHELEINE: (*Beat.*) No one likes the cold nights. If
I didn't know better, I'd say this snow's in to stay. Have
you seen it outside?

KATHRYN: She lives...?

GENEVIEVE: Only five minutes away –

MICHELEINE: Her husband was –

GILMA: ...The nuts are finished.

MICHELEINE: ...a marvellous man.

GENEVIEVE: He died...

GILMA: Four years ago...

MICHELEINE: He painted the picture as a memory for us
all.

GILMA: Under-wired, most definitely. With stockings and
suspenders.

MICHELEINE: La Perla have the ones I normally prefer.

GENEVIEVE: (*To MICHELEINE.*) Have you called
   Angelica? (*Beat.*) Micheleine? She's at home with the baby
   boy?

MICHELEINE: Your accent it's...?

GILMA: Californian.

GENEVIEVE: California?

GILMA: Hollywood.

KATHRYN: Hollywood, my arse.

GILMA: It's beautiful.

KATHRYN: She's making chitchat.

GILMA: You've worked in America?

KATHRYN: Elections, a race riot, some bomber in Idaho,
   some coverage in South America. The Idaho bomber a few
   years ago.

GILMA: Idaho?

KATHRYN: In America.

GILMA: Yes, Hollywood.

KATHRYN: A1 wonderful. An interpreter who doesn't
   actually know how to interp. (*Beat.*) She's not even
   listening.

GILMA: (*Beat.*) I hear every word.
   (*GILMA knocks her drink back too hard, coughs.*)

MICHELEINE: Careful –

GILMA: It just catches you –

MICHELEINE: ...when you're least expecting –
   Chilli, chilli vodka.

GILMA: Right at the back of /

MICHELEINE: ...the back of the throat.
   (*MICHELEINE hands her a glass of water.*)
   (*Beat.*) Alright now?

GILMA: Thank you.

MICHELEINE: You're welcome.

GILMA: That's quite alright.

GENEVIEVE: (*I.e. drink.*) ...Micha, where did you get this?

MICHELEINE: (*Beat.*) Lunch with Isabella. (*Beat.*) She
   insisted. She insisted I bring a bottle home.
   'For the pain. The chilli? To enjoy the pain as you drink it.'

I knock back the last mouthful quickly, gently scalding
my tongue. We won't forget this moment. We want you
to know this. There's a sincerity that embarrasses me.
Embarrasses my husband.
I pray he does not intervene with another joke.
Help me out, sweetheart. We have a little signal –
'Darling, your ulcer? We must get that ulcer home.'
My husband informs us, our car is surely waiting. It is as
we leave I notice –

•

(*GILMA is standing admiring a beautiful Venetian vase, red
and lilac catching in the light, roughly wrapped in newspaper
and rolling on its side.*)

GILMA: It's beautiful.

(*MICHELEINE nods.*)

MICHELEINE: Venetian.

GILMA: The vase?

MICHELEINE: In Isabella's hallway, resting on a bookshelf. A
wedding present we gave them some years ago.

KATHRYN: She nods so lightly –

GILMA: So carelessly forgotten.

MICHELEINE: Isabella is a woman who guards possessions
carefully.

KATHRYN: ...roughly wrapped in newspaper and rolling on
its side.

MICHELEINE: I am therefore surprised when she takes it
down from the shelf and offers it to me.

GILMA: A vase which I can see is worth half of what
I earned last month. A vase which, at this moment,
I would dearly like to own. Red. Venetian. She's clearly
distracted... I wonder if she'd notice –

MICHELEINE: (*To GILMA.*) A gift.

(*GILMA leans forward to touch the vase, turns, aware of
MICHELEINE watching her, withdraws her hand.*)

'Take it – we'd like you to have it.' Is it my imagination or
does our hostess shake as she holds it out in her arms?

GILMA: ...It would fit in my coat.

MICHELEINE: My smile is a graceful smile but as we stand in her hallway I see there is pity in her husband's eyes.

(*The phone starts ringing.*)

Marianna, our –

GILMA: (*To KATHRYN.*) ...housekeeper –

MICHELEINE: Don't worry, she normally answers it.

(*The phone stops ringing.*)

KATHRYN: That noise? What is it?

MICHELEINE: There's no breeze. The silence carries everything.

GENEVIEVE: The door was wide open, I didn't think of closing it, I thought she must be outside –

MICHELEINE: I forgot. (*Beat.*) It's her half – day.

He squeezes my hand and leans back to kiss me. Tells me that there are papers at the office that he really must sign. I am to go on alone, he'll be back quite shortly. I clutch the half bottle of vodka and the vase from these strangers. People we have known and loved for years.

Something about his manner. Something about his manner... We pull through the gates and...

•

KATHRYN: We are here when she arrives.

(*MICHELEINE stands, a drink somewhere near. GILMA is once more on the floor sweeping up some glass with a dustpan and brush. KATHRYN is standing looking at the painting. GENEVIEVE now has her coat on, her hair still wet, pulling off her scarf. The repeat is as before only slightly faster.*)

MICHELEINE: Genevieve. (*Touching hair.*) Your hair, it's –

KATHRYN: ...dripping on her green dress.

GENEVIEVE: I'm fine. The roads are terrible.

MICHELEINE: It's nothing, just a bit of glass. (*Introducing.*) Gilma –

GENEVIEVE: Gilma.

GILMA: Don't look me up and down like that.

GENEVIEVE: I had to take the back route. Is there anything to drink?

MICHELEINE: Yes, we're onto our third…

(*MICHELEINE offers KATHRYN a cigarette.*)

Do you mind?

(*KATHRYN shakes her head.*)

I'm giving up.

GENEVIEVE: Jesus, where did you get this?

MICHELEINE: Isabella.

GILMA: Marlboro. A brand new pack.

MICHELEINE: Genie, what are we to do with you? I'll get you a towel.

•

KATHRYN: She is shorter than I expected and not as beautiful, certainly not as her photos have shown. Her behind is large and there is a thin line of hair bleached on her top lip. Her clothes are too tight and the handbag that she is carrying –

MICHELEINE: Prada. Last season's and shoes to match.

GILMA: Pink with tiny stripy edging. The soles look barely dirty. I pray. Yes indeedy they are my size. (*To MICHELEINE.*) Your shoes, they're very hairy.

KATHRYN: Animal not mineral. Possibly Zebra.

GILMA: She says she thinks you're wearing –

MICHELEINE: (*To GILMA.*) I really don't think so.

KATHRYN: If there's a seam, tell her, it's normally where the anus once was.

GILMA: (*To MICHELEINE.*) She likes them.

MICHELEINE: Please tell her thank you, I have many more.

KATHRYN: Amidst such devastation how do you…

GILMA: Devastation… To cause great destruction…

KATHRYN: (*Beat.*) I barely embarrass her.

GILMA: They're delivered by road.

KATHRYN: How many handbags –

MICHELEINE: …do I actually own? (*Beat.*) A number is not important.

GILMA: I'm glad I've worn my big coat, with very, very deep pockets.

MICHELEINE: A figure is just a crude way to define us all. I find it rather tasteless... This fascination with quantity.

GILMA: Twelve in each side and one larger pocket just under my arse.

MICHELEINE: Two maybe three...hundred. (*Beat.*) She asks too many questions. I grace them by –

KATHRYN: ...showing us the room where they are stored.

MICHELEINE: How can you quantify something that means nothing to one person and everything to another? A number is redundant.

•

MICHELEINE: (*To GENEVIEVE.*) I've been showing them my handbags.

(*KATHRYN's gaze falls to the painting beyond.*)

KATHRYN: On the wall is a painting. An obscene and gross painting. It is modern. In oils. Smeared like shit.

GENEVIEVE: (*Beat.*) I see you've noticed the painting, the painting on the wall?

KATHRYN: Gilma, can you tell her, the light, it's fading.

MICHELEINE: (*Beat.*) My husband... Will you explain to her...

GILMA: At the office...

KATHRYN: Yeah. I got that.

MICHELEINE: He's had to –

KATHRYN: ...sign papers. Yeah. She said that before.
(*Watching MICHELEINE.*) Her nails are aubergine, the colour of aubergine, and clasped around her bag even in her house. As if she is under threat, as if she is under threat or about to go somewhere.

GILMA: (*To GENEVIEVE.*) Fuck, you're freezing?

GENEVIEVE: My heating's jammed –

MICHELEINE: That car –

GENEVIEVE: It's a bit temperamental.

MICHELEINE: Genie, it's time to get rid of that car.

GILMA: ...You drove along the...

GENEVIEVE: Past the Gymnasium...

MICHELEINE: The changing rooms are now offices and the athletic pitch barracks...

GENEVIEVE: Since they bombed the bridge last August –

GILMA: ...It's the only route to take.

GENEVIEVE: (*To KATHRYN.*) Your first time here? Over here?

MICHELEINE: You must visit our coastal towns.

KATHRYN: (*To GILMA.*) I've been mainly...mainly in the Northern states.

MICHELEINE: (*To GENEVIEVE.*) Gilma's the interpreter, if you want to talk to –

KATHRYN: (*As if introducing herself.*) Kathryn.

MICHELEINE: ...Kathryn, Genie, it's best if we all go through her.

KATHRYN: The piano?

MICHELEINE: My grandson –

GILMA: (*To KATHRYN.*) ...has lessons here.

MICHELEINE: Tuesdays and Thursdays.
What am I doing? Shut up. Stop talking so much.

KATHRYN: I'll have to move it. The piano. Gilma?

MICHELEINE: (*To GILMA.*) Ask her, will you ask her...will I see the pictures first?

GILMA: The pictures, you'll send copies?

KATHRYN: The film will go on the first flight. I don't get to see –

MICHELEINE: He has a little disfigurement to the left of his face –

KATHRYN: The film goes ahead of me.

MICHELEINE: ...he's naturally self-conscious. The removal of a mole.

GILMA: Shoot him from the left.

KATHRYN: It will depend on the light.

MICHELEINE: He's a man you admire?

KATHRYN: More fascinated.

GILMA: More fascinated.

MICHELEINE: (*Beat.*) To me he's my husband. The piano...
Be careful. It is a Steinway.

(*A sound. Faint. Just audible. In the distance. Bells/shelling/ the rumble of guns.*)

He squeezes my hand and leans back to kiss me. A small patch of stubble... Back in one hour. Just give them a drink – Oolio... Oolio... He's already gone.

(*To GILMA.*) Your English. You learnt?

GILMA: In the University of California.

GENEVIEVE: California?

MICHELEINE: (*To GILMA.*) You're very lucky...

KATHRYN: California my arse. (*Watching MICHELEINE.*) She's nervous.

MICHELEINE: I'm shaking. The hostess' disease. The young girl is sly, her coat is quite terrible –
The older. Tougher. No ring. No man.
Kathryn, it is Kathryn who clocks my hands. God I need a drink.

KATHRYN: We move the piano.

MICHELEINE: Careful –

GILMA: We make a big great scratch as we drag it across the floor. If we're moving pianos I'm asking for more.

KATHRYN: On the stool is an imprint, a perfect crease, a perfect crease of a very tiny child's behind.

GILMA: Her grandson's.

MICHELEINE: He's this tall. A sweetheart. A tiny little sweetheart.

(*The ring of a phone. For a long time until –*)

Excuse me, a moment –

KATHRYN: She answers the telephone.

MICHELEINE: (*As if on the phone.*) Darling...

GENEVIEVE: She's talking to Oolio.

MICHELEINE: And ruining my floor. (*As if on the phone.*) She seems very nice. She's brought a lot of equipment. (*She laughs.*) I'll tell her... I'll tell her... (*To KATHRYN.*) He's making a joke.

GENEVIEVE: She laughs too much.

MICHELEINE: I laugh too much.

GILMA: Something funny at his office.

MICHELEINE: He says would you mind...

GILMA: Would we mind holding on?

•

(*MICHELEINE pours three shots for them. They all chink glasses and knock back in one shot.*)

KATHRYN: Wow.

GILMA: Jesu –

MICHELEINE: I'm sorry I should have warned you.

KATHRYN: I like it.

GILMA: (*Coughing.*) Jesu –

KATHRYN: (*To GILMA.*) Are you okay?

MICHELEINE: The first time I tried it, my husband had to slap me, hard.

(*MICHELEINE hits GILMA between the shoulder blades.*)

I'll get you some water.

GILMA: It catches you –

MICHELEINE: Right at the back of –

GILMA: ...the throat.

(*MICHELEINE hands her a glass of water.*)

MICHELEINE: (*Beat.*) Alright now?

GILMA: Thank you.

MICHELEINE: You're welcome.

GILMA: (*Beat.*) Nice glasses.

MICHELEINE: Siberian.

KATHRYN: (*Eyeing GILMA.*) I know what you're doing.

GILMA: (*Holding up glass.*) M for Micheleine.

MICHELEINE: A whim of my husbands. M on all the silverware.

GILMA: (*Admiring the glass.*) M that's very nice. If I could just get a set.

KATHRYN: Put it back, put it back, put it back –

•

KATHRYN: Her children?

GILMA: They live near.

KATHRYN: The grandson with –

MICHELEINE: My daughter, Angelica.

GENEVIEVE: The girl translates.

MICHELEINE: ...touches everything.

GILMA: (*Beat.*) She's married to an obstetrician.

MICHELEINE: My son is studying –

GILMA: …at agricultural college –

MICHELEINE: …in the North. My daughter, Angelica, she lives on the Southside. How's Darius?

GENEVIEVE: Skiing. He's skiing with a new girlfriend.

MICHELEINE: (*Beat.*) A girlfriend. At last. We had money on it he was…

KATHRYN: The woman flinches.

GILMA: (*To KATHRYN.*) A daughter, a son, one grandson and the woman in the green dress –

GENEVIEVE: Two boys. They're all grown up –

GILMA: They don't live at home.

GENEVIEVE: Have you called Angelica? Micheleine? Is she at home with the boy today?

GILMA: Two glasses. A lighter. Nail varnish and a light thing.

MICHELEINE: Don't worry so. Don't worry so.

GILMA: (*To GENEVIEVE.*) The bells on the Southside. I heard them. This afternoon.

MICHELEINE: Where are you? You worry too much.

GENEVIEVE: (*To MICHELEINE.*) There were people, they were dancing and soldiers being paraded. If Angelica –

MICHELEINE: There is mud on my carpet.

GILMA: (*Picking up soles of feet.*) Fuck… You can't have not heard it.

KATHRYN: …Gilma, your shoes…

MICHELEINE: Outside…outside…

KATHRYN: Gilma –

(*GILMA exits as if going outside.*)

GENEVIEVE: There have been bells ringing all day on the Southside.

KATHRYN: Excuse me…do you mind?

(*KATHRYN holds up her mobile, as if about to make a call.*)

MICHELEINE: Genie, you exaggerate.

GENEVIEVE: The roads… There's a log-jam.

MICHELEINE: You're always prone to exaggerate.

GENEVIEVE: If Angelica's on the Southside…

(*KATHRYN on mobile.*)

GILMA: Inside, I can hear them talking, she is on the
 telephone... Screeching down the telephone. That woman,
 that woman has a pickle up her arse.

KATHRYN: Nick, it's Kathryn... Nick...can you hear me?

GILMA: In the taxi, on the way here I take her the
 long way.

KATHRYN: (*As if on the phone.*) It's the signal... Fuck it...
 I'm here... We've arrived... We're waiting for him...
 Apparently he's on his way... Nick... There's a lot of noise
 coming from the Southside.

GILMA: Down the main street there are fronts of houses, with
 no rooms only doorways. A boy, too big, too old sleeps in
 a pram in a hotel front door.

MICHELEINE: I am nervous. I talk.

GENEVIEVE: Too much.

KATHRYN: (*As if on phone.*) Nick... I can't hear you... Nick...
 Nick... No, he hasn't arrived yet...

GILMA: At a time like this I think of just leaving them.
 The wife is rude, the other doesn't give a fuck. It is only
 a moment and then I remember... The glasses and the
 knives and spoons engraved with the M.

KATHRYN: Nick will you listen... The Southside. There's
 noise coming from the Southside. It's okay...? You sent
 Makin? You sent fucking Makin?
 (*GILMA comes back in.*)

GILMA: Who's fucking Makin?

KATHRYN: (*As loses signal.*) I'm stuck here and fucking
 Makin's on the fucking South – Fuck.

GENEVIEVE: Kathryn, my mother's name.

KATHRYN: I'm sorry. I don't understand.

GENEVIEVE: (*Gesturing.*) My mother? Katerina. It's actually
 the same name.

KATHRYN: Your mother? Right. It's common. I imagine the
 world over. My mother's was Margaret.

GENEVIEVE: Sorry. I don't understand.

GILMA: In a bin, by the window there's an old MacDonald's
 bag. Brown with the M – Millennium.

MICHELEINE: My grandson. Yesterday. He just loves
MacDonald's.

GILMA: And *Toy Story*. On the table. Now in my coat.
(*A sound. A bang. Shelling. Fireworks. Something. Somewhere.*)

MICHELEINE: The windows are open. It feels very cold in
here.

KATHRYN: Micheleine –

MICHELEINE: I'll close them.

KATHRYN: Ask her –

GILMA: Outside. Do you know what is going on outside?

GENEVIEVE: There must be a certain kind of –

GILMA: (*To KATHRYN.*) ...professional ambition, she's asking –

GENEVIEVE: (*To KATHRYN.*) ...I expect it's dangerous –

KATHRYN: (*Eyeing MICHELEINE.*) She's shaking...

MICHELEINE: I'm shaking. I can hardly close the window.

GENEVIEVE: ...especially abroad. To be so eager to get your
pictures in the papers.

MICHELEINE: If there's no wind, even the river sounds...
sounds not far away.

KATHRYN: (*To GILMA.*) Tell her, I haven't really ever
thought about it before.

MICHELEINE: But you've travelled here, a long way? That
shows a certain passion, a certain belief to do, what you
do?

KATHRYN: In the Northern states I took a photo...there is an
old man. He is holding up a baby. The baby has no eyes. I
suppose... Tell her, yes, I guess yes.

MICHELEINE: Gilma. (*Beat.*) You're not married yet?

GILMA: I'm waiting. For someone to come back.

MICHELEINE: A soldier?

GILMA: A soldier.

MICHELEINE: That's marvellous. That's marvellous.

GILMA: Before I was a lecturer, in science, in physical
science. Before all this happened...

MICHELEINE: And look at you now.

GILMA: (*Beat.*) She patronises me.

MICHELEINE: I'm getting drunk.
That's clever. You are obviously very clever. You can't
quite hear it... Your accent? Am I right?

28

GILMA: My accent?

MICHELEINE: Its Northern edge. You've softened it. Smoothed it over.

GILMA: I don't think so. I've been here a long time.

MICHELEINE: A long time. (*Beat.*) I mustn't have any more. (*Beat.*) I don't like to tell her but she has my *Toy Story* in her pocket.

(*KATHRYN holds up her bag to MICHELEINE.*)

KATHRYN: Is it okay, if I...? Gilma?

GILMA: Is it okay? To unpack her things?

MICHELEINE: Please tell her – (*Calling out.*) Marianna... Will she need some help?

(*KATHRYN shakes her head. She begins to unpack her things.*)

(*Eyeing GILMA.*) I could possibly negotiate. Appeal to her better nature. It is the favourite film of a very little boy but –

GENEVIEVE: It's the view from our window. Not everyone can see it. It's...

KATHRYN: Abstract.

GENEVIEVE: Exactly. Not everyone gets it. It was painted by my husband when he was –

GILMA: (*To KATHRYN.*) ...still alive. He was found... How do you say?

MICHELEINE: Excuse me a moment.

GENEVIEVE: Tell her, he'd been depressed for a very long time.

MICHELEINE: (*Calling out.*) Marianna. Marianna. We need more ice.

(*MICHELEINE walks across the room, ice bucket in hand in search of some ice. She suddenly stands as if she is on the telephone.*)

(*Beat.*) Genevieve?

•

MICHELEINE: Genevieve, just listen for a moment, listen and I will tell you as best I can.

KATHRYN: Somewhere, in a different house, in a different street not far away, this woman in her green dress is summoned to the phone.

MICHELEINE: Genevieve?

GENEVIEVE: Micheleine, you've caught me watching the television. That thing where –

MICHELEINE: Of course. Come over right now.

GENEVIEVE: ...the man wins a million?

(*GILMA touches KATHRYN's camera equipment.*)

MICHELEINE: Don't be silly. That would be fine. Genie.

KATHRYN: It's clear, she's bluffing it...

GENEVIEVE: Micheleine, are you listening? Who are you talking to?

MICHELEINE: There's a lady from the press and we're having a few drinks. He's not back yet... Uh, you know how his work is?

(*KATHRYN puts out one hand to stop GILMA picking up a lens.*)

KATHRYN: Excuse me...

GILMA: Sorry.

KATHRYN: It's just the grease from your fingers. We all have it and don't know it. It smudges the lens.

GILMA: What's this?

KATHRYN: A light meter.

GILMA: What's it do?

KATHRYN: It measures light. It says the light's fading.

GILMA: She looks at her watch.

MICHELEINE: (*As if on the phone.*) You wouldn't be interrupting. We'd love you to come round...

GENEVIEVE: Micheleine and I have been friends for...

MICHELEINE: Twenty –

GENEVIEVE: ...five –

MICHELEINE: ...years... We believe in the same things. Our children...

GENEVIEVE: ...don't get on.

'Micheleine, I'm in the middle of making supper... Micheleine...'

MICHELEINE: She's very lonely. Her husband...

GENEVIEVE: She's been very good to me. She's been very kind to me.

MICHELEINE: Sometimes I have to fight to get the time on my own. Sometimes she calls and I don't want to talk to her sometimes...but today...she's my very best friend.

•

KATHRYN: Your husband was a painter?

GENEVIEVE: At the local art college...

MICHELEINE: Our husbands were school-friends, that's how we met. Tell them the story of the first time you visited...

GENEVIEVE: Micheleine...

MICHELEINE: A dinner party, the first we ever had...

GENEVIEVE: In that flat...

MICHELEINE: Above the butchers. We were so poor...

GENEVIEVE: Scrag end of lamb...

MICHELEINE: And after someone had brought a bottle of...

GENEVIEVE: Pie-eyed...

MICHELEINE: Pie-eyed...

GENEVIEVE: From some grass...

MICHELEINE: My father's place in the mountain... My brother and I used to...

GENEVIEVE: Dry it in their loft... And later... When most of the others had gone home...

MICHELEINE: We danced with each other because our...

GENEVIEVE: Preferred to talk...

MICHELEINE: They hated it most when we would giggle...

GENEVIEVE: ...while they talked rubbish late into the night.

MICHELEINE: How can you say that?

GENEVIEVE: This is where we differ...

MICHELEINE: My husband never talked an ounce of rubbish in his life...

(*A ripple of laughter broken only by the smash of glass.*)

•

(*GILMA stands with pieces of the broken vase in her hand. A silence broken only by the ring of the phone. MICHELEINE lets it ring for some time until –*)

GILMA: I'm sorry. It was just... In my hand.

MICHELEINE: Venetian.

GILMA: I'm sorry.

MICHELEINE: I bought it with my husband, on an official visit abroad...

GENEVIEVE: A gift which she gave to our friend Isabella, a gift now returned to her.

MICHELEINE: 'But Isabella.'

She silences me. This woman gives me back a vase, this woman does not want anything of us.

Don't drink so much. Don't drink so much. Get a grip get a...

I'll see if I can find Marianna. (*Calling out.*) Marianna. Marianna, excuse me please –

(*MICHELEINE goes as if to answer it.*)

GILMA: Christ.

(*GILMA bends down to pick up the pieces of broken glass on the floor.*)

MICHELEINE: (*As if on the phone.*) Hello... Hello...

(*MICHELEINE hangs up returning, bearing a dustpan and brush, handing it in passing to GILMA.*)

•

MICHELEINE: Genevieve –

(*GILMA bends down and starts to sweep up the broken vase as GENEVIEVE stands once more in familiar pose, pulling the scarf off from around her neck. The repetition is faster, now slightly more fragmented.*)

GILMA: ...hair dripping –

KATHRYN: ...green dress.

GENEVIEVE: The roads are –

KATHRYN: ...terrible.

MICHELEINE: Snow –

(*GENEVIEVE looking at GILMA as she sweeps up on the floor.*)

Just a bit of glass. (*As if introducing.*) Gilma.

GENEVIEVE: Gilma.

(*GENEVIEVE waves away MICHELEINE as she goes to take her coat.*)

Don't...

GILMA: ...look me up and down like that.

GENEVIEVE: Micha... Micha... Is there anything to drink?

MICHELEINE: We're onto our third. How's Darius? And Marcus?

GENEVIEVE: He called only last week. He's going to bring...

(*GENEVIEVE walks across the room and pours herself a glass of vodka. The phone rings.*)

Jesus –

KATHRYN: Chilli vodka. In the house of an important man.

MICHELEINE: Lunch with Isabella.

GENEVIEVE: You saw her?

MICHELEINE: A few hours ago. (*Beat.*) You're freezing. What have you – ?

GENEVIEVE: ...lying in the snow.

MICHELEINE: I'll get you... I'll get you... I'll get you a towel.

(*MICHELEINE exits in search of a towel. The phone stops ringing.*)

KATHRYN: This man that I've come to see, this man is a general, a man who is now on the edge of defeat. This man is a figure who fascinates, appallingly fascinates, this man, is now, too many hours late.

GILMA: (*To MICHELEINE.*) I'm sorry.

MICHELEINE: (*To GENEVIEVE.*) Sit down sit down. I hate it when you hover... We thought by the window. Sitting at his desk.

GENEVIEVE: Sorry... Sorry...

KATHRYN: He sends fucking Makin. Scandinavian. World Service. Blonde. Too blonde. With some work done to her lips.

(*They sit. A silence. Time ticks by.*)

GENEVIEVE: Well this...

KATHRYN: Yes...

GENEVIEVE: This is... Very exciting... (*To GILMA.*) She
must visit our –

KATHRYN: Northern States. I cover mainly the Northern
states.

GENEVIEVE: ...coastal towns. It's very exciting to have a
visitor from abroad...

MICHELEINE: Genie, don't embarrass yourself. You're
gushing.

GENEVIEVE: You're drinking too much.

(*GENEVIEVE comes up to look at the painting with
KATHRYN.*)

(*To KATHRYN.*) I see you've noticed the painting.

KATHRYN: Sorry?

GENEVIEVE: The painting? The painting on the wall?

KATHRYN: I'm sorry... (*To GILMA.*) Gilma?

GENEVIEVE: Does she like it? Can you ask her? What does
she think of that painting?

(*KATHRYN looks directly at GENEVIEVE.*)

KATHRYN: When you go to countries where terrible
things have happened, things that I cannot mention,
things that I prefer to look at through the eye of a lens,
when you go to these countries the thing that shocks you
is that you are so shocked you are not shocked at all.

(*The phone rings.*)

MICHELEINE: (*Calling out.*) Marianna...

GENEVIEVE: My husband painted –

MICHELEINE: (*Beat.*) I forgot, today is her half day.

(*No one answers it.*)

KATHRYN: Then something throws you, some incongruous
object, a child's rubber ring or a school book in the mud,
or a grown man crying because he can't get a jar open, a
jar of honey which he has found in the wreck of his house.
You are touched for a moment by the horror of it all and
you close the door quickly, you close it because you can't
look...

GILMA: She wants to know what you think of the painting.

KATHRYN: That painting...that painting is the foot in the
door.

(*A beat. The phone stops ringing.*)

GENEVIEVE: What did she say?

GILMA: Not much at all.

MICHELEINE: Someone will have answered it.

GILMA: (*To KATHRYN.*) Someone will have answered it.

KATHRYN: Gilma, I need to get over to the Southside.

MICHELEINE: (*Beat.*) My husband had he not joined the
 political arena may have been an architect...

GILMA: (*To KATHRYN.*) A builder...

KATHRYN: I'd like to use the phone?

MICHELEINE: (*Beat.*) My daughter. My grandson they live
 on the Southside.

GILMA: (*Holding up video.*) *A Bug's Life.* Second favourite after
 *Toy Story.*

KATHRYN: Cartoons. Fuck. Fuck.

GILMA: Could I watch?

MICHELEINE: If you'd like –

KATHRYN: No.

MICHELEINE: She's rude. So sharp. Why are you so rude?
 They're being rude to me.
 Oolio, where are you? Sweetheart, where are you?

KATHRYN: She tells us the story of the first time she met him –

MICHELEINE: I was standing in the library. He kissed me
 on my neck. Have I told you this story?

GENEVIEVE: No darling, you've not told me.

KATHRYN: She has... Several times... It is clear on the
 woman's face.

GILMA: (*As if to KATHRYN.*) Her husband made love to her –

MICHELEINE: ...around the great buildings of our city...

GILMA: (*As if to KATHRYN.*) Fish markets...and how do you
 say...the place where you...watch the sharks swim.

KATHRYN: Aquarium.

GILMA: Aquarium.

KATHRYN: How unusual...

GENEVIEVE: Yes...

GILMA: I guess yes.

MICHELEINE: (*To GILMA.*) I'm watching you.

GILMA: Amazing, how they get the bugs to talk like that –

MICHELEINE: She thinks that they're real. Christ –

GILMA: She thinks I think they're real. Christ –

GENEVIEVE: (*To GILMA.*) Kathryn, with your work? You
must have travelled?

MICHELEINE: Genie, don't bother her –

KATHRYN: All the time she is talking –

MICHELEINE: ...my husband always says busy people find
it boring to discuss work.

KATHRYN: ...her skin is pulling tighter across her mouth,
and tiny specks of powder blot the beads of sweat around
her nose. The light has now quite gone, I am resigned to
lamplight and whatever I can find.

MICHELEINE: We thought by the window.

GENEVIEVE: Micheleine. It's nearly ten o'clock –

MICHELEINE: Please don't ask – Please don't ask again.

KATHRYN: ...and we've been here since four.

GENEVIEVE: When Micheleine calls I am not watching the
TV programme. The one where the man wins a million.
I am sitting in my kitchen. I have turned all the lights off.
It is dark and outside...the noise is lighting up the sky.
Somewhere there are people smashing shop windows.
And upstairs my neighbour has just hit his wife.

MICHELEINE: Genevieve?

GENEVIEVE: 'You've caught me watching the television.
That thing on the television?'

MICHELEINE: Of course. Why not come over?

GENEVIEVE: 'The one where the man wins a million?'

MICHELEINE: No, that would be fine. That would be
absolutely wonderful.

GENEVIEVE: 'Micheleine...'

MICHELEINE: (*Beat.*) There's a lady, she's here from
the press.

GENEVIEVE: I put down the phone and sit for several
minutes. Upstairs I can already hear someone moving
out. They are filling their car with as much as they can
carry. Knowing that their Northern neighbours may no
longer be their friends. I listen as they bump a washing
machine down the stairs. I wonder what I'll take.
Certainly not a washing machine and suddenly I realise
I'm not going anywhere.

'Micheleine, of course, of course I'll come over.' (*Beat.*)
Twenty –

MICHELEINE: … five –

GENEVIEVE: – years is a long time to despise your best
friend. (*To KATHRYN.*) Why do you look like that?

KATHRYN: Ask her, ask her how her husband died?

GILMA: (*To GENEVIEVE.*) Beautiful colours.

GENEVIEVE: Sorry?

GILMA: (*To GENEVIEVE.*) She thinks beautiful colours.

GENEVIEVE: That's not what she said.

KATHRYN: It's clear he's not coming.

MICHELEINE: I assure you. I assure you…

GENEVIEVE: Will you calm, Micheleine? Calm.

MICHELEINE: His ulcer is grumbling and he's waiting for
some papers. There are some papers he said he has to
sign.

GENEVIEVE: (*Beat.*) Feed them. It's suppertime. They're
probably hungry.

GILMA: She says that she's starving.

MICHELEINE: (*Eyeing GILMA.*) It is you who is starving.

GILMA: There is fruit and some cheese and some left
over cuts.

(*The sound of footsteps as though someone is walking down a
long silent corridor.*)

MICHELEINE: I walk down the corridor to the ground
floor kitchen. I notice that the lights have not been turned
on in the west wing behind. The darkness is surprising,
unfamiliar, unordered. It is ten and by ten, there should
be every light on in the house. In the kitchen I still hope
to find Marianna. (*Calling out.*) Marianna. (*Beat.*) She
normally stays until we are all fed. The oven is off, the
larder is empty, she has even taken the flour and sugar
from the jars. (*Beat.*) I forget, it's her half day. I scrabble…
I scrabble together some kind of supper… Some cheese,
some oranges and there is some fat pork at the back of the
fridge. I arrange them on a plate, as best I can. I walk back
along the corridor. I see fires burning far away, lighting my
route back.

(*Whispering.*) Oolio… Oolio…

KATHRYN: She calls out a pet name.

(*KATHRYN is suddenly standing as if in her path, making MICHELEINE jump, almost laugh, her phone in her hand.*)

I can't get a signal.

MICHELEINE: Christ... Christ... You made me jump.

GENEVIEVE: How old are you?

GILMA: Twenty-four. I know I look older.

GENEVIEVE: No...

GILMA: Yes, I do. I know this. You don't have to lie.

(*KATHRYN and MICHELEINE hover, as if one doesn't know if the other should cross their path.*)

KATHRYN: Can I try it in here? (*As if entering a room.*) Wow...

MICHELEINE: For state entertaining. For official visits.

KATHRYN: Oolio?

MICHELEINE: A pet name. I thought I heard him come back.

KATHRYN: Outside, Micheleine? You are aware of what's going on the Southside? My office says there are riots building up over there.

(*MICHELEINE turns and heads back as if with the others.*)

MICHELEINE: I am aware of the young Northern girl, Gilma, as she wipes her plate with the skin of an orange, eating the peel to get the last of the grease.

GILMA: Jackie Collins? My God, I love Jackie Collins.

MICHELEINE: I am aware of my best friend, my dearest friend, Genevieve who is trying to make conversation, trying to make everything alright...

GILMA: Second shelf. Lady Boss... American Star is her best.

MICHELEINE: I am aware of something happening outside of here, I can hear the noise, I just chose to lie. My husband, he finds them relaxing. I prefer...

GILMA: Shakespeare. The complete works...

(*As GILMA licks the last of the food off the plate with her fingers.*)

MICHELEINE: Please mind the china. The plates are a set.

GILMA: (*Holding glass.*) Nice glasses.

MICHELEINE: Siberian.

KATHRYN: I can see one in your pocket. I'm not an idiot. Put it back.

MICHELEINE: Gilma has a boyfriend. A soldier.

GENEVIEVE: That's very nice.

(*KATHRYN picks a book off the shelf, puts it back.*)

KATHRYN: Lady Boss. Sometimes there are pockets of
insight that one can't help but try and shoot.

GENEVIEVE: A soldier?

GILMA: The State Military.

GENEVIEVE: That's admirable. A soldier –

MICHELEINE: Gilma's from the North.

(*A long silence.*)

KATHRYN: Your phone, may I use it?

GILMA: Where is your telephone please?

KATHRYN: Mine can't get a signal.

MICHELEINE: Left. Then right. Then left again.

(*KATHRYN goes to use the phone.*)

GILMA: The woman in the green dress watches me while
I finish my food up. It is obvious what she is thinking. 'Her
manners? Of course she's from the North.' I eat the orange
peel not because I have to, not because I am in poverty but
because I like the taste.

KATHRYN: I get through to the office. The line is faint.

GENEVIEVE: Your accent?

GILMA: It's been five years.

GENEVIEVE: You've visited your family?

GILMA: No. Not often.

GENEVIEVE: That's a pity. I couldn't live, I really couldn't
without mine.

MICHELEINE: Liar.

They've never actually visited her. I love Genevieve. She's
my very, very best friend but sometimes… I won't say this
until we are alone.

GENEVIEVE: I'm sorry.

GILMA: Sorry? What is there to be sorry about?

KATHRYN: (*As if on phone.*) Nick… Nick… Which bridge?
Which bridge? I can't walk… It's freezing… Are you going
to get me a taxi…? Nick. It's not happening…
It's just not happening. We've been here since four,
because the light has gone.

GILMA: I visit my family, one day last summer. They ask me how I am. I can't bear the way they eat. I show them the clothes and the things that I have brought them. A jacket from Marks and Spencer's. A video – a hip and thigh diet for my mother. 'Hip and thigh...hip and thigh...where is the food for me to get fat?' This is said, so that I send more money for them each month. 'Even in a war you must make the effort... Even in a war, mother...' Even in a war, I polish my shoes.

MICHELEINE: Gilma has a boyfriend. A soldier.

GENEVIEVE: That's very nice. A soldier? I hope you love him very, very much.

MICHELEINE: You –

GILMA: ...plan to get married when he gets home.
As soon as I say this, I wish that I hadn't. Not because I am lying but because it was never true.

KATHRYN: (*As if on the phone.*) ...I don't know what's going on here. I don't know why I'm here. Nick, don't piss around. I don't know what to do now. You sent Makin.

GILMA: Fucking, fucking Makin.

KATHRYN: (*As if on the phone.*) Fuck you. Fuck you. Yeah fuck her too.

GILMA: She swears a lot. (*Beat.*) Her office is telling her to stay where she is.

KATHRYN: (*As if on the phone.*) He may have asked for me but he's not fucking here.
(*KATHRYN, as if slamming down the phone.*)
Gilma, the taxi. We can we get the taxi?

GILMA: We said not until later. We have to wait.

MICHELEINE: My husband has a driver. Perhaps I could call him.

GILMA: She makes gestures to find her diary and call her husband at work.

GENEVIEVE: Your work must be fascinating you take photos for a living?

MICHELEINE: Genie, don't bother her. Oolio says busy people don't like talking about work.

KATHRYN: In places of crisis –

MICHELEINE: My favourite of us is at Christmas...

KATHRYN: ...places of war.

GENEVIEVE: And you're not frightened? You're not moved by the things that you see?

KATHRYN: I'm sorry? I'm sorry?

GENEVIEVE: You don't understand at all.

MICHELEINE: It was taken last year. Christmas. With all of us. The family.

GENEVIEVE: Micha, have you called Angelica? Is she at home with the boy?

(*MICHELEINE goes and pours herself another drink.*)

KATHRYN: On the desk is a photo. Of her husband with his family. He is wearing a paper hat, he is flushed, the hat's awry, like a comical drunkard or a man with one eye. There is a smile on his face and clasped around wrinkled fingers are those of his grandchild hugging the skin... He's very...

MICHELEINE: Like his grandfather... Do you have children?

KATHRYN: No. Not at all.

MICHELEINE: (*To KATHRYN.*) Are you married?

GILMA: She's asking if you are...

KATHRYN: No.

GENEVIEVE: I imagine there is no time...no time with your work...

KATHRYN: Sometimes it is easier if I say I am married. Sometimes it is easier...

MICHELEINE: *Bug's Life.* Now also stolen. Slipped in her jacket. *Toy Story* in her pocket. *Bug's Life* most probably wedged under her bra.

This portrait of my husband? This portrait that you plan to take? You must be important. He rarely courts press.

KATHRYN: It was agreed through my office. A request from his advisors.

MICHELEINE: He's a man you admire?

KATHRYN: More fascinated.

GILMA: More fascinated.

MICHELEINE: To me he's my husband.

KATHRYN: And to the rest of the world?

(*The phone rings. And rings until – it stops.*)

GILMA: ...You drove along the...

GENEVIEVE: Past the Gymnasium...

GILMA: As a child I used to swim there. I taught there for two semesters. Before they... I was there the day they filled in the pool.

MICHELEINE: The changing rooms are now offices and the athletic pitch barracks... We needed headquarters. (*Beat.*) I suggested it one evening after supper in bed.

GENEVIEVE: She wants us to admire her.

KATHRYN: In this light she is almost bearable.

MICHELEINE: By morning there were engineers knocking down walls.

GILMA: Your husband used to go there?

MICHELEINE: He'd been depressed a long time.

GENEVIEVE: With my children.

MICHELEINE: Don't upset her.

GENEVIEVE: Marcus is twenty-one. Darius our youngest is almost eighteen.

MICHELEINE: You've heard from him?

GENEVIEVE: Last week. A painter like his father. He's been skiing for the winter.

MICHELEINE: She is lying.

KATHRYN: She is lying.

GENEVIEVE: He's met a new girl. He doesn't say exactly but as a mother you know.

MICHELEINE: Genevieve.

KATHRYN: The look on her face says she is desperate for us to believe her. The look on her face knows we suspect it's not true.

MICHELEINE: (*Beat.*) A girlfriend. At last. We had money on it he was...

GENEVIEVE: My husband used to tease him. He is gentle like his father. (*To GILMA.*) You don't have children?

GILMA: No. Not yet...

GENEVIEVE: And you?

KATHRYN: No, not at all.

MICHELEINE: (*To GENEVIEVE.*) It's a joke. Don't look so serious. You take me far too seriously.

KATHRYN: (*Watching GILMA and GENEVIEVE.*) She offers her an orange. The woman in the green dress.
(*The phone rings. MICHELEINE eventually gets up to answer it.*)
MICHELEINE: Hello. (*Long silence.*) Don't do that darling. (*Breaking into a long broad smile.*) He's teasing me on the telephone... We're eating... Only cold cuts... (*Calling out.*) We'll leave some for you.
GENEVIEVE: As we drink the last of the vodka, her comment still burns me. You may have had money on it Micha, but I know my son is not gay.
MICHELEINE: All the time that I am talking they shell oranges on my floor.
KATHRYN: All the time that the wife is talking, the lady in the green dress is pulling a thread from the corner of her skirt.
GILMA: It's lovely... It's lovely... That green is a lovely colour...
GENEVIEVE: You think so?
GILMA: I think so...
(*MICHELEINE laughs, still on the telephone.*)
(*Eyeing GENEVIEVE.*) She has five notes in her purse. A bus ticket and a library card. And a photo of a man, he is eating a hunk of sausage and standing with a watering can, squinting in the sun.
GENEVIEVE: My husband was fascinated with light and how it fell on life... His paintings were also the balance of dark and light...
KATHRYN: You're crying.
(*GENEVIEVE gets up to pour herself another drink.*)
You're crying. You're trying not to show us. But as you pour yourself a drink, there are tears in your eyes.
(*GILMA touching KATHRYN's camera equipment.*)
KATHRYN: (*To GILMA.*) Don't do that... Please don't do that... You keep on touching...
GILMA: Sorry...
KATHRYN: If you keep on touching you'll get grease on the lens.
(*MICHELEINE enters as if off the phone.*)

MICHELEINE: He asks that you leave him some of the ham, please. It's his favourite, his sister sends it from her own farm.
She stares at me. I turn and catch her eye, aware she's always watching me.

KATHRYN: You don't look...

MICHELEINE: Forty-five, forty-six next month.

KATHRYN: She's a vain woman. This flatters her.

GILMA: She says you don't look it... She says...

KATHRYN: Tell her she has beautiful skin.

MICHELEINE: That's really very nice of you... That's really very kind of you...

GILMA: I take the five notes and a photograph.
(*MICHELEINE walks across the room, takes a packet of cigarette, lights one.*)
I slip the purse of the green lady back in her bag.

GENEVIEVE: In my house I have several photos. Of Micheleine with my family. Micheleine and him and my husband and me. On boating trips and birthdays and there is even one at my husband's memorial. Micheleine sitting, head bent down at her husband's side.

KATHRYN: She has this way of turning her head, as if trained, as if knowing that this is captivating...

GENEVIEVE: The photo was commented upon, noted, that they both visibly cried.
(*To anyone.*) I have the most marvellous photo of Micheleine at my home.

MICHELEINE: There's an edge in her voice.

GILMA: She says she has a photograph of Micheleine at her husband's funeral.

KATHRYN: She barely can look at us. She can barely believe she's said it.

MICHELEINE: Have you, Genie? I don't think I've seen that one.

GENEVIEVE: I always admired the coat you wore.

MICHELEINE: You can borrow it...
(*GILMA scoops the vase up in her hand, holds it.*)

KATHRYN: I don't need to understand to understand.

MICHELEINE: ...any time at all.

•

(*GILMA stands listening as the vase breaks. A silence broken only by the ring of the phone. MICHELEINE lets it ring for some time until –*)

GILMA: I'm so sorry. It was just… In my hand.

MICHELEINE: (*Calling out.*) Marianna… Marianna… I'll get you. (*Calling out.*) Marianna… I get you… I'll one minute… (*Going.*) We need more ice.
(*MICHELEINE scoops up the ice bucket to go and get more ice. The phone stops ringing.*)

GENEVIEVE: I climb into the car and bolt the gate behind me. My neighbour has many possessions littered across the grass. A washing machine, a wheelbarrow, a bed, a table… 'You should think of leaving. They won't want you staying here.' I chose to ignore him. I'm not ungracious. I'm not unfriendly. As I pass in the car, I see his dog sleeping in the machine's metal drum. I drive along North route and past the Gymnasium. I stop. I lie in the snow too long. I think of going to sleep. After, the streets are already littered and there are several broken panes of glass. Someone has set off a burglar alarm and there is a crowd near the crossroads. I lean forward and lock my doors. I take the back route here. I drive through the gates and already I know it is over. Maybe now my sons can come back.
(*MICHELEINE enters, back with a fresh ice bucket of ice, passing the dustpan and brush to GILMA.*)

•

MICHELEINE: Genevieve –
(*MICHELEINE stands. GILMA is once more on the floor sweeping up some glass with a dustpan and brush. KATHRYN is standing looking at the painting. GENEVIEVE now has her coat on, her hair still wet, pulling off her scarf as if she has just arrived. The repetition is faster, fragmented into a ricochet of words.*)
Hair…

GENEVIEVE: Snow.

(*GILMA sweeps up on the floor.*)

MICHELEINE: Venetian... Special vase –

GENEVIEVE: The roads...

KATHRYN: Green dress.

GENEVIEVE: Oolio –

(*MICHELEINE offers KATHRYN a cigarette. KATHRYN declines. GENEVIEVE pours herself a glass of vodka.*)

MICHELEINE: Onto our third.

(*The phone rings.*)

Genevieve. Kathryn... Gilma... Best to go through her. You're freezing...

GENEVIEVE: The heater on my car packed up...

KATHRYN: You have a car?

GENEVIEVE: Very old. Very battered.

MICHELEINE: I am shaking. I am frightened. I want to tell them I am very, very frightened. I had not planned for this. What happens next?

GENEVIEVE: Micheleine, there is trouble –

MICHELEINE: I was telling them how we first met.

GENEVIEVE: As far as the North route.

MICHELEINE: The military?

GENEVIEVE: Are not around.

MICHELEINE: Hair...

GENEVIEVE: ...dripping.

MICHELEINE: Towel...

(*MICHELEINE goes to get GENEVIEVE a towel. GENEVIEVE watches KATHRYN looking at the painting. The phone stops ringing.*)

GENEVIEVE: (*To KATHRYN.*) The view from our window... From our house... You see? That is the river and that is the persons...

KATHRYN: And which bit are people?

GENEVIEVE: You see their faces?

KATHRYN: Your husband painted?

Your husband painted it?

For them?

(*GENEVIEVE nods.*)

GENEVIEVE: (*To GILMA.*) Tell her, will you tell her, I find it frightening too.

(*MICHELEINE enters and drops the towel into GENEVIEVE's lap.*)

GILMA: They are talking about the painting. All three standing in front of it. That is when I take *A Bug's Life*. That is when. When their backs are all turned. Earlier Kathryn has asked her –

(*A sound. A bang. Shelling. Fireworks. Something. Somewhere.*)

KATHRYN: The noise?

MICHELEINE: It's much louder if you have the windows open.

GILMA: She closes them. Ignores our gaze. I translate of course.

MICHELEINE: On a clear day…

GILMA: When there's no wind…

MICHELEINE: You can hear almost everything. The silence carries everything.

GENEVIEVE: When the children were younger you could sometimes hear them splashing no matter how far you were from the swimming pool.

(*MICHELEINE takes the towel, rubs GENEVIEVE's hair.*)

MICHELEINE: Genevieve. Don't gush now. What are we to do with you?

(*GENEVIEVE hands back the towel to MICHELEINE.*)

Help me, Genie, help me. I don't know what to do.

GILMA: (*Watching MICHELEINE.*) She's frightened. You can see this. She smiles but she is frightened. Her mind is elsewhere. She won't notice what I take.

MICHELEINE: When I pick up the phone, the first time there is no one. The silence is empty but there is definitely someone there… The second time I can hear them talking in the other room…

GENEVIEVE: My husband was fascinated with light and how it fell on life…

MICHELEINE: She's trying to impress them, flaying around in artist talk…

'Hello.' (*Long silence.*) 'Don't do that darling.'

Someone is sending insults down the line... Terrible words cutting through the silence –

'Bitch. Whore. This is the end.'

A Northern accent. (*Breaking into a long broad smile.*) He's teasing me on the telephone.

KATHRYN: Most times when you are working there is no time to set your photo. You don't want to, you shoot it just as you see...

(*A sound. A bang. Shelling. Fireworks. Something. Somewhere.*)

GILMA: Bang.

(*A ripple of laughter as GILMA makes them laugh.*)

MICHELEINE: A noise. Like gun fire.

I am worried because I think I hear a young boy crying. I am worried because...

(*Beat.*)

My daughter... Angeli...lives on the Southside.

KATHRYN: If you keep on touching you'll get grease on the lens.

(*MICHELEINE, as if re-entering the room.*)

MICHELEINE: He asks that you leave him some of the ham, please. It's his favourite, his sister sends it from her own farm.

GENEVIEVE: Micheleine...

MICHELEINE: It wasn't him... It was someone... I don't know who it was... It was someone...

GENEVIEVE: How did they get your number?

MICHELEINE: I don't know... I don't know...

GILMA: If I hadn't been a lecturer, I might have been a photographer...

KATHRYN: People always say that...

GILMA: Do they? I wonder why.

GENEVIEVE: Call him.

MICHELEINE: I have tried. I don't even get his secretary.

GENEVIEVE: Do you think?

MICHELEINE: No.

GENEVIEVE: Do you think maybe...

MICHELEINE: No.

GILMA: Buzz Lightyear is not real, he's an electronic space
man and the cowboy...he's the hero. He doesn't like it
when he moves in on his patch.

MICHELEINE: What are they talking about?

GENEVIEVE: They're making conversation.

GILMA: The cowboy is in love with... I can't remember who
the girl is.

KATHRYN: Barbie?

GILMA: Of course, Barbie, but she is the fantasy, the cowboy
has a real love that the space man steals.

KATHRYN: This is a ridiculous conversation... This is a
fucking ridiculous conversation...

MICHELEINE: Bo Peep. It's Bo Peep. I've watched it with
my grandson.

GILMA: Of course it all turns out alright in the end.

KATHRYN: The wife is upset. She is being hushed by the
woman in the green dress. (*To GENEVIEVE.*) You're
freezing...

GENEVIEVE: The heater on my...

KATHRYN: Could you drive me, if I paid you, over to the
Southside?

GILMA: On the Southside is the flat where I live with my
boyfriend's mother. She is poor and I work to make sure
there is money coming in –

GENEVIEVE: The North route is log jammed...

KATHRYN: But there's a road, we drove past it...

GENEVIEVE: I can't.

KATHRYN: Please –

GENEVIEVE: Don't ask me. I can't.

MICHELEINE: She can't. Alright? Alright.

(*Beat.*)

GILMA: This morning I receive a call from my agency. There
is one phone in the hall, which you can only use at certain
times in the day. I am told I am to come to interpret for the
wife of a diplomat and a journalist, a photographer who is
coming into town. Giving the taxi driver instructions which
I have picked up from the agency, it is only then I realise

where it is we are to go. He is not just a diplomat, he is more than a diplomat. My mother-in-law is excited.

MICHELEINE: Gilma's from the North.

GILMA: I decide not to lie.

GENEVIEVE: Your accent?

GILMA: It's been five years.

GENEVIEVE: You've visited your family?

GILMA: Sometimes.

GENEVIEVE: (*To KATHRYN.*) I'm sorry. I can't. The roads are too icy.

KATHRYN: Snow.

GILMA: Snow, slowly falling outside.

(*The four women stand as if looking out of the window, watching the snow fall as it floats by outside.*)

GENEVIEVE: The night my husband died –

MICHELEINE: You were having supper with us...

GENEVIEVE: He had gone to take the children to the Gym –

MICHELEINE: And left her all alone. I persuaded you to come and eat with us... Our husbands were school friends, that's how we met. Tell them the story of the first time you visited...

GENEVIEVE: Micheleine...

MICHELEINE: A dinner party, the first we ever had...

GENEVIEVE: In that flat...

MICHELEINE: Above the butchers...

GENEVIEVE: Pie-eyed...

MICHELEINE: Preferred to dance...

GENEVIEVE: ...while they talked rubbish late into the night...

MICHELEINE: This is where we differ... My husband never talked an ounce of rubbish in his life...

(*GENEVIEVE gets up and goes to look out of the window.*)

KATHRYN: Maybe if I could take the car. I have an international driver's licence.

MICHELEINE: And insurance? You have the right kind of insurance? I didn't think so. That would be dangerous.

KATHRYN: In times like these –

MICHELEINE: Have you no family? Someone you should think of. Have you no one who may be worried about you back home.

GENEVIEVE: I don't think it would get you there.

KATHRYN: It is no more dangerous than what is going on in here. Translate it... Gilma will you please tell her what I said?

GILMA: The car's fucked. Don't keep asking. I've paid for the taxi. To take us back to the Southside.

(*KATHRYN looks to GILMA who remains silent until –*)

She says that is fine. She will wait for the taxi ride.

(*MICHELEINE nods, offers KATHRYN another orange from the bowl... KATHRYN hesitates then takes it and starts to peel, she walks as if going outside.*)

GENEVIEVE: Fireworks.

(*KATHRYN nods. They look up as if above the sky has just lit up.*)

KATHRYN: Fireworks. And not even November...

GENEVIEVE: Sorry...

KATHRYN: It doesn't matter.

GENEVIEVE: I'm sorry. I don't understand.

KATHRYN: Sometimes, tonight, I wonder why I do this.

GENEVIEVE: I loved my husband.

KATHRYN: Sorry?

GENEVIEVE: Love. I loved my husband.

KATHRYN: I'm sorry? I don't know what you're saying.

GENEVIEVE: I want you to know that.

KATHRYN:  I don't know...

I'm sorry.

GENEVIEVE: You don't need to understand to understand.

(*GILMA peels an orange.*)

MICHELEINE: There's a bowl...

GILMA: She is watching even when I peel an orange.

MICHELEINE: Why don't you put your peel in the bowl?

GILMA: Sorry. Sorry.

MICHELEINE: There's no need to be sorry... (*Beat.*) Your boyfriend, the soldier, is he from the North?

GILMA: His family live here, here in the city.

MICHELEINE: I thought not. I thought not in the army. If he was from the North, they wouldn't let him in.

(*GILMA pauses in peeling her orange, letting the peel drop to the floor.*)

KATHRYN: How far away? (*Beat.*) The noise? The light?
I was wondering how far it was actually away? It's getting
nearer.

GENEVIEVE: (*Looking at KATHRYN.*) I wonder, looking at
this woman, if this was a different time, if we spoke the
same language, if this hadn't happened, if I wasn't me and
this all hadn't happened, would we be friends?

KATHRYN: The light. It doesn't matter...

GENEVIEVE: She carries a kind of melancholia... Your
family?

KATHRYN: Family. Just me. Not really any family.

GILMA: What are you fucking looking at?

GENEVIEVE: A kind of melancholia that is familiar to me.

MICHELEINE: *Bug's Life* in your coat. Don't think
I haven't noticed, Gilma.

GILMA: Shit she's going to say it.

MICHELEINE: Gilma (*Long silence.*) you've some orange in
your teeth.
(*GILMA picks, nods. Silence.*)

GILMA: Your husband is a great man.

MICHELEINE: To me he is my husband.

GILMA: My boyfriend has his picture above our bed.

MICHELEINE: He's a soldier. As it should be.

GILMA: Yes of course, as it should be –
(*MICHELEINE holds out her hand. GILMA disposes the
peel into her hand.*)
Thank you.

MICHELEINE: You're welcome. Gilma.

GILMA: Gilma. Micheleine.

KATHRYN: The woman in the green dress is shivering...
Genevieve?

GENEVIEVE: Genevieve.

KATHRYN: You're shivering... We can go inside.
(*GILMA flicks through one of the books on the shelf.*)

GILMA: Are you not worried about your husband?

MICHELEINE: Are you not worried about your soldier?
(*GENEVIEVE puts out a hand as if stopping KATHRYN.*)

GENEVIEVE: Kathryn?

KATHRYN: Kathryn. She puts out her arm. Stops me.

GENEVIEVE: Kathryn.

KATHRYN: Holds me with her look.

GENEVIEVE: Don't be like me.

KATHRYN: What are you saying?

GENEVIEVE: I lay in the snow tonight and I wanted to sleep.

KATHRYN: I'm trying to understand what you are saying.

GENEVIEVE: Don't go. I have to tell you...

> (*MICHELEINE rolls back laughing as if GILMA has just told her the funniest joke.*)

MICHELEINE: (*As if bursting into conversation.*) That is the rudest joke that I ever heard.

GILMA: He learned it in the army.

MICHELEINE: And it best stay there. We thought that you had gone...

GENEVIEVE: I was showing her the car.

KATHRYN: She's right, I can't drive it.

GILMA: The car is fucked.

KATHRYN: That's not what I said.

GILMA: She says you're right, she can't drive it. But thanks very much.

KATHRYN: If you are going to talk for me can you try and get it right.

GILMA: If you don't speak it how do you know what I am saying?

> (*The phone rings. MICHELEINE does not move.*)

If you don't speak it how do you know what I am saying?

KATHRYN: I know.

GILMA: Pardon. (*Beat.*) You don't speak a word.

KATHRYN: Tell her I'm concerned her husband isn't coming, tell her...

> (*The phone rings some more. GENEVIEVE goes and answers it.*)

GENEVIEVE: (*As if on the phone.*) At last... This isn't good enough... You have us all waiting... I'll tell her but she won't like it... (*Calling out.*) At least another hour... (*As

*if into the phone.*) Yeah, yeah, yeah… This isn't your wife
you're talking to… (*Laughing.*) You listen, that kind of talk
doesn't wash with me…
(*GENEVIEVE, as if coming back off the phone.*)
That man I tell you is such a trickster, Micheleine, he tried
to seduce me right under your nose… He promises kisses
and sends his apologies. Less than an hour. (*To KATHRYN.*)
Thirty minutes at the most.

MICHELEINE: You spoke to him. He's on his way, Genie –

GENEVIEVE: Yes, I spoke to him. Apparently the papers have
only just arrived, he'll be here as soon as he's signed.

MICHELEINE: Did he give you a message? Did he not want
to speak to me?

GENEVIEVE: No.

MICHELEINE: No?

GENEVIEVE: No.

Is there any more to drink?

The photograph. Where did you find it? In your hand?
The photograph?

GILMA: Under your chair. It must have slipped…

GENEVIEVE: Out of my bag. Marcus is twenty-one. Darius
almost eighteen. There's a new girl. He doesn't say exactly
but I know –

MICHELEINE: (*Beat.*) A girlfriend. At last. We had money
on it he was…

GENEVIEVE: Gay. You're going to say he is gay. No. You
always say that but no you are wrong.

MICHELEINE: What do I say? Genevieve, if I have
upset you…

GENEVIEVE: You haven't but let us now at last set the
record straight. My son is not gay. My son is gentle. My
son is like his father, but for you it is easier to say…

MICHELEINE: Genie –

GENEVIEVE: Easier to say…

(*GILMA stands up and moves across the room, placing back
the video of 'Toy Story' onto the table.*)

GILMA: My favourite is *Bug's Life* –

KATHRYN: She places it on the table. She is totally
unashamed. The wife and the woman, the lady in the
green dress, stop their arguing, the wife is momentarily
bemused...

MICHELEINE: My grandson's.

GILMA: And there it is back. (*To MICHELEINE.*) Your
husband is a man I admire, Miss. Your husband is a man
who I believe is doing good. Your husband, I am grateful
to your husband for all he has done –

MICHELEINE: For your people? For your family?

GILMA: My family is not my family. My family is my soldier.
My family, like your husband, despises people from the
North.
My mother says 'A soldier? You are sleeping with a
soldier?' 'Yes, mother. Yes, mother. What is wrong with
that?'
One day through her door my mother gets a tongue, cut
out from the throat of my brother, her youngest son.

MICHELEINE: That's most surprising. I'll tell my husband.
He will be surprised to find that...you...feel the same way.
Well done.

GILMA: Bloody and dirty and staining the newspaper it's
wrapped in. A dirty Northern tongue. A warning to us all.
You're welcome.

MICHELEINE: That's quite alright.

GILMA: What?

KATHRYN: In a Northern town not far away, an old man
brings me a baby, a baby that the soldiers have gouged the
eyes out from.

GILMA: What?

KATHRYN: The old man is holding the baby up to me to
witness, holding it up, asking me to take it, to take it in
some way.

GILMA: What?

KATHRYN: I feel sick. I feel sick, not because I have not seen
this before, because I have just used the last of my film. I
pretend to this man. I shoot anyway.
You're from the North.

GILMA: I'm whatever I want to be. In my pocket, is your
    licence. International. EEC. (*As if reading.*) Kathryn
    Margaret Foxton. Kate Foxton.
KATHRYN: Give that back.
GILMA: It fell out in the taxi. You might need it when you get
    home.
KATHRYN: I'm going to tell the agency. Not to use you
    again.
GILMA: That is fine. That is fine. I can always find work
    elsewhere.
KATHRYN: And after. Where do you go then? When your
    soldier is back? What happens then?
    (*A sound. A bang. Shelling. Fireworks. Something. Faint.
    Yet closer than before.*)
KATHRYN: Did you hear that? What's happening?
GILMA: Sssh... The snow is blanketing the noise.
KATHRYN: (*Watching MICHELEINE.*) Lamplight.
    A window. The back of... She leans out... Her feet hang.
    Her nose pressed. Hard against the glass. The sound of...
    Somewhere... The snow keeps falling.
MICHELEINE: When I first met my husband, my father did
    not want us to marry, it was all a secret, I used to meet him
    at an old school hall outside of the town. One winter, when
    the snow was so thick that for days we would never leave
    the house, only my father would be picked up and driven
    to work. The days were very boring and my sister was so
    irritating and all I wanted to do was see him, this boy, who
    I did not yet know whether I loved, when there was a tap
    at the window and I looked down and it was him and I
    say... 'Ssh my little sister will give us away.' 'Don't worry
    my darling, no one will know that you have been with me,
    walk in my shoe steps, follow behind me and then there
    will be only one set of footprints in the snow.' So I followed
    him through the dark of a very, very short day and that
    afternoon, while my sister played house with my mother,
    we made love for the first time until I was sore –
    He leans back to kiss me. A small patch of stubble.
    Something about his manner. Back in one hour.

I feel sick.

Genie, I'm rambling –

GENEVIEVE: It's late...

MICHELEINE: Did someone win a million – ?

GENEVIEVE: No, a fat lady had trouble with a question on the pope.

MICHELEINE: Did you know the answer?

GENEVIEVE: No.

MICHELEINE: You must read more, Genie, you really must read more.

(*A beat.*)

GENEVIEVE: New handbag.

MICHELEINE: Last season's.

GENEVIEVE: It doesn't look it.

MICHELEINE: You're sniping...

GENEVIEVE: I'm not, Sweetheart.

MICHELEINE: You're picking a fight.

GENEVIEVE: Micha, when I drove over, I saw they had firebombed the Southside.

MICHELEINE: Along the Terra –

GENEVIEVE: Yes –

MICHELEINE: Oh my God...my God...

KATHRYN: If I told you how many people were covering this catastrophe, if I told you how many people were probably over on the Southside...

GILMA: What do you want me to do about it?

What do you want me to do about it?

You're here now. You have to make the best of where you are.

Fuck Makin.

KATHRYN: Scandinavian. Working for the World Service press. National Geographic... Definitely, most definitely has had work done to her lips.

GILMA: You've not had sex, it's clear –

KATHRYN: Piss off.

GILMA: ...in a very, very long time.

KATHRYN: Is swearing not universal?

GILMA: Desperate.

KATHRYN: Fuck you. Is that nice and clear?

GILMA: When? One year...two...

KATHRYN: Three... Three months ago...

GILMA: Not bad. And you enjoyed it?

KATHRYN: Laughing. Teeth rotten. Orange caught in her gums. Yes I enjoyed it.

GILMA: (*Sniff.*) I sometimes get it wrong.

KATHRYN: Brief. Necessary. Uncomplicated. Uncommitted. Men like me. There's not a problem. Men like me for that.
(*GENEVIEVE comes through holding a coffee tray.*)

GENEVIEVE: I'm afraid there's no milk but (*Holding up a bar of chocolate.*) I found this treat.

KATHRYN: Thank you... Thank you...

GILMA: Is Micheleine alright?

GENEVIEVE: Her daughter she lives –

KATHRYN: With the boy?

GILMA: With the boy...

KATHRYN: Your family?

GILMA: ...your family?

GENEVIEVE: ...moved away when their father –

MICHELEINE: (*As if on the phone.*) As I ring the office...
The woman who finally answers is my husband's secretary. She spent last Christmas here when her house was burgled and she had nowhere to go.
'Where's Oolio...? He's not there? But he was coming to sign papers. He was coming to you to sign papers. But he's taken the car... There's noise. A lot of noise.'
(*The woman hangs up on MICHELEINE or is cut off. MICHELEINE takes the cup of coffee proffered in GENEVIEVE's hand and drinks.*)
See, he's on his way.
(*Aside to GENEVIEVE.*) He didn't call. You didn't talk to him –

GENEVIEVE: Micha –

MICHELEINE: Why did you lie?

GENEVIEVE: Did you want me to tell you that some man with a thick Northern voice, a thick Northern gruff voice, a thick angry Northern gruff voice thinks you're a whore?

I thought not. (*Beat.*) I thought not.

MICHELEINE: It's the waiting.

GENEVIEVE: Yes... I know... I understand that.

(*MICHELEINE suddenly breaks into a low, wailing,*
*engulfing outpouring that shocks and silences those around her,*
*for several seconds until, regaining composure* –)

MICHELEINE: No milk? The milk is on the sill. I put it there
this morning. Excuse me...

KATHRYN: No one says anything until –

(*The clitter-clatter of heels as if disappearing down a long*
*corridor.*)

MICHELEINE: I have never noticed until this day what a
clitter-clatter my tiny mules make along this corridor.
I have never noticed the way my husband winces every
time I run to greet him, fuss around him, scoop the work
papers out of his arms and ask him to tell me about his
day. 'Darling, your shoes.' I thought it was just him...just
his grumbling ulcer... I thought that my conversation...
my concern...my direction when yet another problem fell
in his lap, yet another blot on the landscape threatened to
disrupt some important advance, soothed this noise. That
my advice, taken, relied upon, needed, often acted upon,
was enough to disguise the clitter-clatter of heels I have
observed in other women.
'Where's Oolio?'
'He's not here.'
'But he was coming to sign papers. He was coming to you
to sign papers.'
'Micheleine, you must get out of the house. Micheleine you
must get a car and get out of the house and get out of the
city as soon as you can.'
'But he's taken the car...'
There's noise. A lot of noise...
'Micheleine. I can't talk to you now. He has left you. He
has left us.'
(*The footsteps stop. MICHELEINE takes the milk and pours*
*it into a jug.*)

KATHRYN: He wasn't on the phone, was he?

GENEVIEVE: No.

KATHRYN: If he has been... If he's left...

GENEVIEVE: I am sorry... I am sorry that you have come all this way... I am sorry –

KATHRYN: What are you sorry –

GENEVIEVE: ...That you have walked into this mess...

KATHRYN: It's my job. This is what I do.

GILMA: Where's he gone?

GENEVIEVE: I don't know.

GILMA: At that moment I see my mother-in-law... My non-mother-in-law, my boyfriend's mother, where I live until my boyfriend comes home...

I kiss him with my dirty Northern tongue.

(*GILMA picks up the vase, once more lying on its side in newspaper.*)

Above his bed is a picture of the general, the husband. At that moment I see my mother-in-law screaming at others to get out. They have stolen her television and are writing things on the wall... The Northern invasion...

It is with my mother-in-law that I have learnt to speak. She turns a blind out to the odd clumsy vowel, I assure her that this is a throwback to some distant relative a long time ago who came from the North side... I know she doesn't believe me but the money I bring in is more important to her. It is I who stole the trainers that she wears on her feet. Nike Air, size seven. Men's. Too big. Uncomfortable. Taken from a journalist who was careless with his bag. If this is it...if this has not been for anything better than this –

·

(*GILMA breaks the vase, looking up as MICHELEINE comes in bearing a dustpan and brush, a jug of milk in the other hand.*)

MICHELEINE: Gen...

(*GILMA bends down and starts to sweep up the broken vase as GENEVIEVE stands once more in familiar pose, pulling the scarf off from around her neck. Language is almost obliterated, the physical actions more important than what is said.*)

Hair...

KATHRYN: ...Dripping...

GENEVIEVE: Kathryn...

(*GENEVIEVE and KATHRYN go to shake hands but stop.*)

KATHRYN: Tell her. Sounds outside. Woman in the green dress... Staring at me... Holding up a baby... Baby crying without any eyes...

Gilma, outside, ask her does she know that outside, the crowd, they'll be seeking a revenge.

MICHELEINE: A number is not important. A number is redundant. What means everything to one person and nothing to someone else.

(*GILMA does not respond.*)

KATHRYN: Gilma?

GILMA: I can't translate that.

MICHELEINE: (*To GENEVIEVE.*) I've been showing them my handbags.

KATHRYN: You won't translate that?

GILMA: I won't translate that.

GENEVIEVE: I think she is questioning whether it is right to stay.

MICHELEINE: (*To GENEVIEVE.*) Did you go? You did not. Even when your husband died. You did not leave. Did you? Did you? Look at your hair.

GENEVIEVE: Why have you stopped crying? I could feel sympathy for you when you were crying. I can remember the warmth of that night when we ate scrag end of lamb and our husbands danced with us and mocked us and laughed at us. And twenty-five years on here we are now.

I think she is right. I think you should go.

MICHELEINE: I'm not listening.

GENEVIEVE: You can hear me.

MICHELEINE: I'm just not listening.

GENEVIEVE: Oolio has left you...

MICHELEINE: (*Eyeing KATHRYN.*) You've been listening too much to her.

GENEVIEVE: On the way here, on the North route I passed the Terra Strata, the road is firebombed, my neighbours were cheering...

GILMA: The Terra Strata. My boyfriend and I live near.

MICHELEINE: How long have I known you? How long have I known you?

GENEVIEVE: Twenty –

MICHELEINE: – five...

GENEVIEVE: ...years.

GILMA: I see my mother-in-law, her hair is on fire.

MICHELEINE: And you give up now... He will not be pleased with you... Don't blame me if Oolio's angry with you...

(*GENEVIEVE gathers together her coat and bag, as if preparing to go.*)

Genie, take your coat off.

(*MICHELEINE picks up a towel and rubs GENEVIEVE's hair.*)

GENEVIEVE: I want to be with my children. If I drive around the back road I might make the Strata route.

MICHELEINE: And you think they'll want to see you? They don't want to know you. I know, Genie, don't make us laugh any more, everyone has always known.

KATHRYN: Woman in the green dress. Almost bent double. Mouth slightly gaping as if she is going to laugh or as if she is trying not to lose the sweet out of her mouth.

Genevieve, are you alright?

(*GENEVIEVE nods.*)

(*To GILMA.*) What did she say?

GILMA: She says –

MICHELEINE: Your sons don't love you. They've lost where they've come from –

GILMA: She says –

MICHELEINE: When was the last time they even sent a card?

GILMA: She says –

GENEVIEVE: You make it hard for me to like you.

GILMA: When did you last see –

MICHELEINE: ...your own grandchild.

I understand why you're angry. I understand that there is jealousy – Your husband is dead while mine is still alive.

(*To KATHRYN.*) Suicide is painful.

GENEVIEVE: It wasn't suicide.

MICHELEINE: Suicide is surprising, but we weren't surprised. (*To GILMA.*) Translate it.
He was a very unhappy man. (*To GENEVIEVE.*) When the inquest was called you were happy to admit this, you were happy to acknowledge that he had not been as well as before.
He had a certain darkness, a way of not seeing the world... It was irritating, destructive to say the least. I've kept the painting as a tribute to him. A reminder, that on every life some rain must fall.
(*To GILMA.*) Translate it.

GILMA: (*To KATHRYN.*) Do you understand?

KATHRYN: Yes, I understand.

MICHELEINE: He'd been depressed. It was clear he'd been depressed for a long time.
(*GENEVIEVE sinks into her chair. MICHELEINE comes over and takes her hand.*)

KATHRYN: The wife, head to head with the lady in the green dress. The loll of a scuffed sandal next to the wife's thin zebra mule.

MICHELEINE: I'm sorry. I'm sorry. Genevieve, I'm sorry, but there was nothing, nothing anyone could do.

GENEVIEVE: She calls me up, and says –

MICHELEINE: Genevieve, get your self up here –

GENEVIEVE: We have oysters to eat. There's far too many, so won't you join us. Bring...

MICHELEINE: (*To KATHRYN.*) Her husband. Her husband was a very good man.

GENEVIEVE: I leave him a note. Say come on later.
He's taken our youngest son to the swimming pool.
Fourteen. Darius is just fourteen.

MICHELEINE: (*To KATHRYN.*) He painted the picture, a commission for my husband. It was meant to be the most glorious view. Instead you give me polemic, instead you give me mind-numbing politics, lies. That painting lies.

GENEVIEVE: I arrive at this house and drink oysters and a liqueur. It goes to my head. I'm almost a flirt. Somebody mentions... 'Your husband is a long time.' I'm happy. Not

worried. He'll be at home with the boys. And when I get
home, the house is empty. The police have called. I'm to
go at once. I arrive at the station to find my youngest sitting
in a waiting room, holding his father's swimming towel.
He drowned. He'd been depressed. He'd taken too
many... I know what pills he takes. No, you're wrong, who
kills himself in view of their child? Takes and swims and
drowns in view of their child. Without me even ringing
them, I look up and see Micheleine and him, and I know, I
see through my youngest's eyes.

MICHELEINE: If we hadn't have kidnapped you. I'm so
sorry, Genie...

GENEVIEVE: My youngest wants to speak, to say something
but I squeeze his hand hard –
No... I was with my friends all night long. I tell the officers.
I see Oolio laughing in a back room with some officers,
some brusque aside, some inside joke, about nothing,
about some man who drank some magic beer and thought
he was Superman, a stupid nervous joke, inappropriate
yet needed, badly timed yet delivered with the telling of a
raconteur, funny, making her laugh. And I know...

GILMA: I was there the day they filled in the pool.

MICHELEINE: There were no headquarters. (*Beat.*)
I suggested it one evening after supper in bed. It seemed
the only tribute to a very dear friend.

GENEVIEVE: She thinks that we admire her.

KATHRYN: In this light she is almost bearable.

MICHELEINE: By morning there were engineers knocking
down walls.
Genevieve, we're not going anywhere. We're here for the
duration.
(*MICHELEINE squeezes her hand, takes her coat.*)
You and I have nothing to be ashamed of.

KATHRYN: Your daughter? She lives on the Southside.

MICHELEINE: No matter.

KATHRYN: But your grandson?
(*A beat.*
*MICHELEINE smoothing across the piano school, as if*
*ironing out a crease, she takes a seat.*)

MICHELEINE: Yes, I hear what you say.

GENEVIEVE: The morning after my husband's funeral, I sit in his studio and I look at the painting and suddenly I see what the rest of the world can see. A frightening view, a view of the outside. Unsettling, mocking, outspoken, outside of what one is allowed to say and I hear Micheleine.

MICHELEINE: But darling, where's the glorious view?

GENEVIEVE: The next day I drive the painting over to Micheleine. 'You must have it. Please take it. He painted it for you.' And I let them comfort me. Let them joke about his outspokenness. Because that painting frightens me, it frightens me like it did them. And from that day I am lost to my sons who see me fawn, and smile, and listen and console with these people so that they can survive. So that I...

In the distance. Shelling. Fireworks. Something. Somewhere. Very distant. Muffled by the snow and the wind and the distance.

GILMA: I look at this woman. I have her bus pass in my bag. And a lip pencil and some tweezers and a small St Christopher.

Cunt bastard's way too late.

(*Looking to KATHRYN.*) Taxi.

(*GILMA knocks back her coffee, slipping the cup and saucer into her bag. GILMA exits as if waiting for the taxi. MICHELEINE sits on the piano stool watching as KATHRYN packs up her equipment.*)

MICHELEINE: Where do you live? At home. Where is your home?

KATHRYN: I'm sorry... I don't understand what you say...

MICHELEINE: It's nice? Your home.

KATHRYN: Gilma...

MICHELEINE: And when you walk in, what do you see?

KATHRYN: I'm sorry... (*Calling out.*) Gilma? Translation please...

MICHELEINE: There is a mirror, and a table, with a key on the table and a vase of flowers, normally fresh, next to a rack of shoes –

KATHRYN: (*Calling out.*) Gilma –

(*GILMA smokes a cigarette, which she has only just lit, admiring the lighter, in her hand.*)

GILMA: My boyfriend is home on leave. We lie in bed and he pulls out the first of my grey hairs. 'Don't go too grey before I get back. Will you marry me?' Yes, I say when you come back and we have a nice house, a video, a Prada handbag. Yes, I'll marry you but looking at this boy, this soldier, with one rotten tooth, from sweet drinks when he was young. I know we won't win. I know he is no hero. I know what he does to the…my…people from the North.

MICHELEINE: When you came into my house you walked along the corridor and there are several prints, cartoons, political, mocking, which my husband likes…

KATHRYN: I don't understand you…

MICHELEINE: A bicycle is always against the door, always waiting for my complaint to Marianna who should have moved it. It is not mine. Turning left is the drawing room and to the right is reception –

KATHRYN: Gilma –

MICHELEINE: I have chosen everything in this house. Everything in this house has a place, has been chosen for a reason, everything I have formed an attachment to.

(*The sound of distant violence. Getting closer. GILMA as if standing in the snow, watching the distant violence coming near.*)

GILMA: I call out 'Kathryn'. No one hears me. The city burns now brightly. Kathryn… (*Calling out.*) Kathryn we have to go soon…

KATHRYN: They will come in this house and they will ransack it and take your things and you know what they will do to you then –

MICHELEINE: You've never looked have you? When you walk in your house, you've hardly noticed what is around, have you?

GENEVIEVE: Micheleine...

MICHELEINE: Have you?

>  (*GILMA enters.*)

> Ask her?

> There's mud on my carpet. Your shoes.

KATHRYN: What is she saying?

GILMA: She is asking about your house. The rooms.

MICHELEINE: I want to know what her house is like, she has come into mine... Ask her. Ask her.

GILMA: She says –

> (*A beat.*)

KATHRYN: Hallway... Lampshade... I don't know...

>  (*To GILMA.*) Will you tell her, I think she should leave now?

MICHELEINE: In the bedroom there's a –

KATHRYN: A bed –

MICHELEINE: (*Beat.*) That is it?

GILMA: (*To KATHRYN.*) That is it?

KATHRYN: There's a lamp and some proofs of photos that I am always about to check.

MICHELEINE: And what is on these photographs?

GILMA: The photos? By your bed?

KATHRYN: I don't want to... I don't... The massacres in the Northern states. There are several photos of children with their wounded mothers. There's a boy with his father.

GILMA: ...They've cut off his hands... Some soldiers, they're taunting a local man, the local man...they're making him kill his dog.

KATHRYN: There's a small shot looks like nothing...

GILMA: Just like a puddle, it's iced over but through the water...

KATHRYN: There's a face...

GILMA: Some kid still grubby from the sandwich he was eating, the morning the soldiers came and burnt his house.

MICHELEINE: Tell her I want her to take a photograph.

GENEVIEVE: Micheleine, I'm leaving –

MICHELEINE: Tell her.

GILMA: You've to take the photo.

MICHELEINE: Tell her I want her to take the photograph of me before and after they come –

GILMA: Before and after they come...

(*A ricochet of noise. Muffled but nearer...*)

MICHELEINE: Tell her, a woman who describes her subject better than her own home, a woman with such attention to detail for her subjects, such an eye for detail, this is a woman after my own heart...

Tell her what does she have left if she doesn't have history?

Tell her I'm a piece of history right under her nose.

Tell her I want her to shoot my right side, even after... My right side is the side I want the world to see...

Tell her outside of history she is nothing... A parasite... I am history... I know what I leave behind...

Tell her I want to be seated in front of the painting... Tell her I take back nothing...

(*From somewhere the phone rings. And rings. And rings. And stops. Silence. GENEVIEVE picks up her coat and bag and makes to go.*)

Genie. Don't drip, sweetheart, you're leaving a trail of water. (*Calling after.*) Be careful. The roads are icy.

(*GENEVIEVE pauses, then walks over to MICHELEINE and slaps her hard across the face. A silence. GENEVIEVE turns and exits.*)

GENEVIEVE: (*Calling back to GILMA.*) You can have a lift if you want.

(*GILMA walks across the room before taking off her shoes and dumping them in the bin.*)

GILMA: Your shoes... A Northerner needs your shoes.

MICHELEINE: Gilma –

GILMA: A Northern name. Did I not say before?

(*MICHELEINE looks down at the mules on her feet, then slipping them off she holds them out to GILMA.*)

MICHELEINE: I think they're your size.

(*GILMA hesitates, then takes them, nods her thanks and exits.*)

KATHRYN: I am sitting in the lobby of my hotel. After.

The taxi driver is arguing. He did turn up last night... He haggled about the money even when all around him...

In my wardrobe there are several packets of linen unopened. This is not some fetish just always the thing I buy. When I find myself walking aimlessly around a department store, normally en route back from some job somewhere, I always buy sheets, or pillowcases, whatever. I always buy clean white sheets. I suppose that's my whim. I take them home and am about to unpack but instead I leave them in the wrapper, for next time. I don't know why. I don't know why. Some kind of comfort I suppose. To know that somewhere they are there.

As we drive to the airport, the taxi driver curses. An old lady dances while a young soldier is shot. He is dragged through the street by a rope by his neighbours, who this week are the ones seeking revenge.

On the plane, they serve pineapple and chicken with thin chips, and for once, I am not hungry. For once I want to go...home.

(*A ricochet of noise. Louder. Nearer.*)

A window. Lamplight. The peel of an orange. The turn of the face as she stands looking out.

MICHELEINE: My face against the light. His book collection in the background. My skin. I have good skin.

(*As if seeing through a window.*) ...The world is white...

KATHRYN: The hallway. The darkness. The door open outside. Outside –

MICHELEINE: The snow. Everything is...

KATHRYN: ...everything is...

MICHELEINE: ...stay and take your photograph

KATHRYN: ...white...

MICHELEINE: What else is there to do?

(*The rhythmic ricochet of noise the silent undercurrent.*)

I am seventeen, it is snowing, I am walking back with... he's ahead of me... I tease him to hurry up, bored with his pace. He is lumbering and frightened of the ice and won't go any faster so I step across him and this time it is he who has to tiptoe behind to match my boot. And he does, laughing. It is snowing, and we are laughing. And that is when I know I have found the love of my life.

Oolio... Keep up.

KATHRYN: I'm sorry. I don't know what you're saying.
  (*MICHELEINE turning slightly to the right.*)
MICHELEINE: My right side...
  (*The ricochet of noise grows louder, carrying the ripples of violence, of shelling as KATHRYN hovers with the camera in her hand, as if holding a gun.*)
  Shoot... Shoot...
  (*KATHRYN hesitates then slowly aims her camera –*)

*The End.*

TENDER

for Jacob

# Characters

TASH
late 20s/early 30s

SQUEAL
late 20s/early mid 30s

HEN
early 30s

GLORIA
mid/late 40s

MARVIN
late 40s/early 50s

NATHAN
mid/late 30s

AL
mid/late 30s

The play is set in a city.
There are several locations.

*Tender* was first produced by Birmingham Repertory Theatre Company with Hampstead Theatre and Theatre Royal Plymouth, at Hampstead Theatre on 6 September 2001 with the following cast:

SQUEAL,  Nick Bagnall

HEN,  Caroline Faber

TASH,  Kate Fleetwood

AL,  David Kennedy

NATHAN,  Sean O'Callaghan

GLORIA,  Nicola Redmond

MARVIN,  Benny Young

Director,  Anthony Clark

Designer,  Niki Turner

# SCENE 1

*Flat, London. Dawn light. SQUEAL in lady's dressing gown, late 20s, peering into a fridge. A wall. A window. Nothing else. TASH, late 20s, enters in towel and shower cap.*

TASH: Back. Second shelf.

SQUEAL: (*Sniffing carton.*) It's off.

TASH: I'm making cheese.

SQUEAL: It doesn't matter.

TASH: It was a joke. (*Beat.*) I don't eat breakfast...

SQUEAL: Squeal...

TASH: Right... Squeal?

SQUEAL: Yeah.

TASH: Weird.

SQUEAL: As in pig.

TASH: Let's try and keep the magic shall we... (*Beat.*) How did you...?

SQUEAL: I was just in the pub and someone said party at...

TASH: (*Pointing to self.*) Veronica's.

SQUEAL: Veronica's.

TASH: My name.

SQUEAL: Liar.

TASH: You been reading my post?

SQUEAL: Only the junk mail, *Veronica.*

TASH: Keep your snout out, *Squeal.*

(*TASH lights a fag. Opens the window and perches on the sill. He stares at her. Too long.*)

SQUEAL: (*Gesturing to fridge.*) Some of the stuff in here...

TASH: Don't tell me...

SQUEAL: What do you live on...

TASH: High finance.

SQUEAL: Yeah?

TASH: I'm actually a broker. There's only two women on our board of directors and you're looking at one of them.

SQUEAL: You never would have –

TASH: I don't look the type do I? I hate the way people make assumptions. Air Nike trainers, you must be Soho in media; suit, shirt and matching metallic tie, you're something stylish in high finance. It's all a load of...

SQUEAL: ...guessed –

TASH: ...bollocks. You know what I mean. And then everyone thinks why then has she never got any money –

SQUEAL: ...considering everything that you said last –

TASH: ...but it costs a fortune to buy anywhere in London even if it is in some rundown Kosher ghetto with no tube line and a hiding to –

SQUEAL: ...last night...Tash –

(*TASH is finally silenced.*)

We didn't do anything.

(*Silence.*)

TASH: You can go home now.

SQUEAL: Nothing last night. Alright? Okay?

(*A long silence. SQUEAL stares at her. Too long.*)

Fine.

(*SQUEAL exits. TASH stubs her fag out on the window sill, thinking on this.*)

TASH: (*Calling out to him.*) You take it too seriously.

(*SQUEAL comes back, dressed and putting his shoes on.*)

You need to work at the pump 'em and dump 'em bit.

(*SQUEAL continues to ignore her.*)

(*A long beat.*) Nothing?

SQUEAL: Nothing.

TASH: (*Beat.*) I'm glad. (*Seeing his face.*) I don't mean to...

SQUEAL: It's nice to meet someone so –

TASH: Honest.

SQUEAL: It's not as if we're – fourteen –

TASH: I wish.

SQUEAL: You're making me feel –

TASH: Say it.

SQUEAL: (*Beat.*) ...like not asking you for that second date.

(*As SQUEAL reaches for his coat, zipping it up and getting ready to go.*)

TASH: Yuri Gagarin. First man on the moon. I remember.

(*SQUEAL continues to get ready, reaching for a motorbike helmet.*)

And then we talked about oceans of water in the space between stars, the kind of soppy bollocks you talk. Squeal is that really your name?

SQUEAL: Yes. Most people call me –

TASH: (*Cutting in.*) And –

SQUEAL: And?

TASH: And you told me about trying to get in the RAF
as a fighter pilot at seventeen only they found out you
were colour blind and green and red are pretty bloody
important if you're going to stop or go and miss a
mountain. The joke about the mountain, it was funny. And
you cried for a week and I said... 'Great pull line, get the
girl everytime...' See. I don't forget. Then after the party...
which was wild...you came on to me...
I fought you off... You said when are we going to fuck.
I burst into tears. My mate, Hen said... I looked like white
trailer trash but it was a fucking fantastic party...
Wasn't it?

SQUEAL: I was in the pub and someone said, 'Party at
Veronica's.' But you weren't going. So I hung about and we
came back and we talked and you drank and...

TASH: And?

SQUEAL: That's it. No fucking fantastic party. (*Beat.*)
Do you want to go out with me again?

TASH: No.

SQUEAL: Right.

TASH: I'll make some tea.

SQUEAL: Milk's off.

(*TASH goes over and opens the fridge.*)

TASH: Have a drink.

SQUEAL: No thanks.

TASH: Have something. You don't have to go.

SQUEAL: What else is there?

TASH: Stay.

SQUEAL: Is this what you do? I stay, you want me to leave. I
leave, you try to keep conversation going.

TASH: Hey, we've just met.

SQUEAL: And you think I'm a mug.

TASH: I don't.

SQUEAL: Yeah you do. That's fine. A one night stand is fine
but –

TASH: But?

SQUEAL: I liked last night. Why don't we –

TASH: No. I like it like this. Have breakfast?

SQUEAL: You don't eat it.

TASH: I could make an exception.

SQUEAL: You started this.

TASH: Where?

SQUEAL: On a train.

TASH: Tube.

SQUEAL: It's dangerous, I could have been…

TASH: I started this on a tube…

SQUEAL: On a tube giving me the eye…

TASH: That is a matter of opinion.

SQUEAL: Giving me the eye…

TASH: A matter of…

SQUEAL: …and wanting me to follow you.

    (*A long beat.*)

    It was a long walk to that pub. I didn't just go for a drink.

TASH: You enjoyed. I thought you enjoyed…

SQUEAL: The intimacy of strangers?

TASH: Stay and we'll have some tea and –

SQUEAL: We'll talk about planets and things we care about and I'll make you laugh and some time very probably as we're really sobering up, you'll cry and I might get a feel and for a moment I'll be everything you want –

    (*SQUEAL stops himself saying something.*)

TASH: (*Beat.*) You've done this before?

    (*Silence.*)

SQUEAL: Look at yourself.

    (*He exits.*)

TASH: Thanks for nothing… (*Calling after him.*) And then what?

    (*TASH watches him go; goes to the fridge, takes out the milk, sniffs it.*)

# SCENE 2

*Office, London. Morning. A table, two chairs. The sounds of the street outside. HEN, early 30s and pregnant, is sitting patiently in front of a word processor as GLORIA, late 40s, stares into space. A long pause.*

GLORIA: I've done this –

HEN: Yes –

GLORIA: I've had to do this several times before.

HEN: Yeah, I know. I bet it's –

GLORIA: Frustrating?

HEN: It would drive me –

GLORIA: It does. It is.

HEN: It's just that going through it all again, might jog something else and gives me a chance to get to know your case.

GLORIA: You're new?

(*HEN nods. Silence.*)

HEN: Take your time.

GLORIA: Tall. Six feet two. Thinning hair, probably greyer now. Blue eyes. Grey suit. With navy mac and briefcase. Obviously things will have changed by now but –

HEN: Obviously.

GLORIA: Date of birth. Fifteenth November '50. Scorpio. Managed own dry cleaning firm. Parents both dead. No family except one cousin, he never really saw. Liked walking, bird watching, odd bit of football. One scar. Thumb. Bread knife. Nearly cut his finger off. Should have got a stitch.

HEN: That's significant.

GLORIA: It's the insignificance of it all actually.

HEN: Right –

GLORIA: I've had eleven months already of this.

(*Silence.*)

HEN: It was a normal day?

GLORIA: Sorry.

HEN: Nothing out of the usual? The insignificance of it all?

(*Silence.*)

I don't mean to offend you, Mrs...

GLORIA: Gloria.

HEN: Gloria... I just meant Mr Tate, Marvin, hadn't said anything out of the ordinary? Nothing alerted you to your husband's disappearance...

GLORIA: That doesn't mean it was as a normal day...

HEN: Of course.

GLORIA: It could never be a normal day. The colour is too bright, the sound turned up too loud and every smell and taste of that day is –

(*GLORIA stops herself, it's still physical this pain.*)

HEN: Imprinted in your mind.

(*Silence.*)

GLORIA: Re-lived.

(*GLORIA looks to HEN. Silence.*)

HEN: I see. Of course.

GLORIA: Do you get training for this job?

HEN: Yes. I'm training at the moment. They need volunteers.

(*Silence.*)

Over ten thousand people go missing every year... fifty-seven per cent of them come back within the first twenty-four hours.

GLORIA: And the other four thousand and...?

(*GLORIA looks at her, looks away, resumes her stare out of the window.*)

One month more and it will be a year.

(*Silence.*)

I don't want to start counting the anniversaries.

(*Silence.*)

I'd like to see the other woman. I normally see the one with glass –

HEN: I'm her cover.

GLORIA: You know I go through this every month? You should have the same people. It's very distressing. It isn't exactly a good advertisement is it? Missing persons and every time you show up the staff have disappeared.

HEN: We're dependent on volunteers. We tend to find people move on if they...

GLORIA: Don't have a vocation?

HEN: Feel they're unable to work within the strictures of the job. Our funds are quite low. There's only so much we can do without...

GLORIA: Any visible signs of a crime, misadventure or injury.

(*HEN stops, takes GLORIA in.*)

HEN: We're happy to co-operate with the police but we don't actually receive any financial support...

GLORIA: Without a full scale investigation.

(*HEN looks up from typing.*)

You've got to do something to kill the time.

(*A long beat.*)

HEN: Children?

GLORIA: Not really.

HEN: Sorry?

GLORIA: That's a blessing.

HEN: I didn't mean –

GLORIA: Why have any more people in pain?

HEN: Mrs...

GLORIA: Gloria.

HEN: Gloria... Are you having counselling?

(*Silence. GLORIA almost laughs.*)

GLORIA: I find swimming helps...

HEN: That sounds good.

GLORIA: He didn't like chlorine. I never went but now...
Something good has come out of something bad.

HEN: Exactly.

GLORIA: Are you going to put that down? About the swimming...

HEN: I don't think it's...

GLORIA: Because perhaps if you could release that sort of information... I've also decorated the hallway. Citrus colours. He liked blues... It might encourage him to come home...

HEN: Gloria...

GLORIA: If he knows the full extent I am going to make my life tick over. Move on. Keep going. That I'm not a responsibility then maybe he'd want to come back...

HEN: A lot of people...

GLORIA: Blame themselves and ask whether there is
  something they could have done?

HEN: Exactly... They feel that...

GLORIA: I was a fantastic wife...

HEN: I'm sure...

GLORIA: The house was always clean, I ironed shirts. I used
  to even run him a bath. It's old fashioned but it's what I
  did...

HEN: It must be impossible to make sense of why he would
  just go like that...

GLORIA: I try to make sense of it every day. Saturday
  was our shopping day and Sundays we'd often go to
  the neighbours... People don't often get on with their
  neighbours... I get on with mine... We got...get on with
  ours...

HEN: Being on your own is very daunting –

GLORIA: You know that?

HEN: If you were married for... (*Reading screen.*) ...twenty-two
  years...

GLORIA: Twenty-three Monday...

HEN: Partners often find in the period of readjustment that...

GLORIA: Please. Don't talk to me like that.

  (*Silence.*)

  I'm actually starting to enjoy it, that's the fear... I'm
  actually finding that it is becoming normal and that's what
  I find frightening... That's what worries me most... That
  if he did come back, maybe I wouldn't want... That's
  why I think it's so important that you release that kind of
  information... Like I've done the garden and the back wall
  was coming down but John from next door has helped me
  fix it and that you just get on. I'm not helpless. If he knows
  that. That I'm stopping needing him... I think he'll come
  back...

HEN: I don't think I can help you here.

GLORIA: There's a slot on TV. With music and they show
  pictures of people missing. People in Christmas hats,
  slightly pissed people or tired people with rucksacks, at
  parties or hugging their mum, and it's the ones who are
  left who they should show pictures of. Photos of them

smiling and on holiday and waving a flag. Photos that say they don't need them. That might jog some memory in the mind of those who have gone. That they had a family and responsibilities...

HEN: Gloria...

GLORIA: That they don't go to bed at night anymore wondering where they are. That at last they have found peace...

HEN: If that were true you wouldn't be here.

GLORIA: Have you ever been left?

HEN: Gloria, I understand how you must be...

GLORIA: Have you?

(*HEN's silence says it all.*)

Then how do you know...

(*A long silence.*)

HEN: If I could just take down some more details.

(*Silence.*)

GLORIA: How many weeks...until your baby?

HEN: A few yet.

GLORIA: That's good. That's lovely. A new life. Congratulations.

HEN: Thanks very much.

GLORIA: That's quite alright.

(*GLORIA looks to HEN. Holds her stare. HEN returns to typing.*)

## SCENE 3

*Loud bar. London. TASH is standing, suit on, glass in hand. Bright lights. Abstract painting. HEN sits gripped, orange juice in hand.*

TASH: And I'm in this bar and I see him and because at that exact moment I am the most interesting woman in the place who understands him. Then I have to go over and say, 'Wotcha' and then I see who he's with and she's really bloody famous and you'd know her...you know that woman who's in that...we saw it...with the...

HEN: Fuck –

TASH: 'Superb' I say... 'You were so gorgeous in that...
It made me and my friend cry.' And she's all fluffy and
preening herself at this and I say, 'I love you...' And him,
fucking famous arty tough looking fart who I will not
repeat...

HEN: Get on with it –

TASH: For fear, he'll stuff me in a tank and pickle me as
'Fucking Pissed Cow dribbling all over my bit of squeeze.'
He looks at me, so fucking mean he was and he says, 'Go
Away' – in a monotone bloody Babylon 5 android sort of
way and I...

HEN: Because you're pissed...

TASH: Because I'm pissed and because I've powdered
my nose far too many times for me to truly justify any
intellectual conversation, proceed to tell him just how
boring I would find myself and what is he doing here?
Because shouldn't he be at home with his wife and child.
And I've really hit a nerve now...

HEN: Tash... What made you say? What made you say –

TASH: 'Go away.' And he pushes me on the shoulder so I
push him...

HEN: You stupid fucking...

TASH: And we end up playing this pat a cake, pat a cake,
melarky and I'm getting more embarrassing and will not
leave them alone. I'm like a limpet, clinging...and I'm not
a clingy person...am I?

HEN: No. You? No.

TASH: So they get up to go and of course I have to follow
because I'm with Magda –

HEN: Bad girl.

TASH: Great girl. Very good for me. I'm with Magda and
she's saying 'Who?' And I say... Fart art who puts things
in pickle stuff and she's reeling now because she's copped
off with Ben behind the bar who's feeding her Sea Breezes
through a drip and cutting up her own lines on the till and
so we have to find him...

HEN: Tash...

TASH: Don't get like that... So she's dragging me around
but I've forgotten him by then and I'm just preying he's
forgotten me so I sit myself down with this tall guy and I
keep saying 'So what's your name?' 'Paul...' 'And what do
you do?' 'I'm a popstar.' 'So what's your name?' 'Paul...'
'And what do you do?' 'So what's your name...?' 'Paul and
I'm a fucking famous pop star,' and he tells me who, that
band, fucking elevator music, what is that band, anyway he
tells me the name of the band and I say, 'Aren't you meant
to be black?' which pisses him off something chronic and
I say, 'Look I'm sorry' and I can't seem to leave him alone
and I tell him I'd be bored with him if he was me and then
I say...

HEN: You didn't...

TASH: I pull out my trump card, the one that normally always
gets them... Because I'm off my rocks the way I was at...

HEN: Diane's wedding...

TASH: ...And by this time I am almost dribbling all over the
carpet... I say to him... 'Look I'm off my tits. I've been
tied up and drugged and made to take copious amounts
of alcohol I didn't really want...don't be rude to me...
Imagine if I was your mother... Imagine if I was your
sister.' And this is it... This is the big whammy, Hen... Are
you ready for it? Look like it then... 'Imagine I was your
sister...' And he looks at me, this super big pop star and for
the first time I see him, I recognise him and I look around
and the place is crawling with Jack shit celebs and me and
he says...

'My sister wouldn't degrade herself like you.'

HEN: (*Beat.*) Oow...

(*TASH knocks back her drink. A pained silence.*)

TASH: You know...It happens. You get over it but I tell you
I still can't listen to their music without feeling physically
sick.

HEN: I'm sorry.

TASH: See that's why I wasn't going to tell you. Because I
knew you'd get upset.

HEN: I'm only saying.

TASH: It's a story. It's designed to amuse.

HEN: It still must have hurt.

TASH: You see that's when I really question our friendship. When you try to do that 'let's tap into the soft underbelly of her mind,' time. It was a laugh. I told you to make you laugh.

HEN: It is funny.

TASH: Then why aren't you laughing? Fat cow.

HEN: Pickled cow.

TASH: It was the drugs...I'd hardly touched a drop.

HEN: That makes it better? Jesus Tash – So?

TASH: What? What are you drinking?

HEN: I'm alright. The other night?

TASH: You're not fucking drinking.

HEN: I'm alright. It's so fucking loud here. Why do you always want to meet where it's so bloody loud?

TASH: I can't wait for you to shit that watermelon. You're boring without a drink in you.

HEN: I'll be up all night. Tash –

TASH: Al keeping you busy.

HEN: Hah, yeah. Al's knackered, he's working on that site, you know that big site –

TASH: How would I know a big fuck off building site?

HEN: Funny. Very funny. We need the money.

TASH: Is that why you're slaving over a hot computer?

HEN: I enjoy my job. I'm doing something worthwhile.

TASH: And I'm not?

HEN: I didn't mean that... But while we're talking about it –

TASH: Fuck off –

HEN: You never settle –

TASH: I'm a late developer.

HEN: You never settle anywhere for more than a few weeks.

TASH: Who would...who would serve deep fried Mars Bars –

HEN: You got yourself into that job –

TASH: ...stay longer than a few weeks...days... I do do...I can do skilled work. I just challenge, getting into the job then –

HEN: Shagging your way out.

TASH: (*Beat.*) What is the crime, I don't see the crime in that?

HEN: What is it... Today... You're so defensive. (*Beat.*) You copped off the other night.

TASH: I'm always copping off the other night. Have a little one? Go on... Why not?

HEN: It stunts the growth.

TASH: Mental growth of the mother if she can't knock back the odd glass of...

HEN: Will you please... Red wine. One glass.

TASH: That a girl!

(*TASH nods to a waiter. Silence.*)

I could kill him. I could honestly kill him. This wasn't meant to happen.

HEN: Will you get over it? I've been with him six years.

TASH: And you were not meant to get pregnant. It's such a cliché.

HEN: You're avoiding the subject.

TASH: I had a fuck. Doctor. Bit lame with his hands. Which is disappointing in a man of medicine. Haven't seen him since the deed. Nothing much to add.

HEN: And I was hoping.

TASH: No please. Shall we go on?

HEN: No. I don't want to get too tired. I promised Al. He worries.

TASH: You promised Al. (*Beat.*) I like Al. I love Al. He's like a brother to me.

HEN: You just get like that. More protectful. More aware... There was a time I would just step out on a zebra crossing even if...especially if I saw a car. I figured the insurance policy would pay for the new leg and the holiday of a life time. It would be worth it but now...

TASH: When you get like this it leaves me cold. I'm sorry.

HEN: You're getting worse.

TASH: I'm definitely getting worse.

HEN: You should have got use to it by now.

TASH: It's a shock.

HEN: What?

TASH: That you're settling... You're choosing to settle. You're having your future now.

(*Silence.*)

It's gorgeous. It's lovely…

HEN: It's normal. Women of our age have children. It's a good age.

TASH: For doing something with your life.

HEN: I don't remember that being single was so great.

TASH: Oow.

HEN: (*Beat.*) Sorry.

TASH: Point deserved. If I could be like you. I don't choose this –

HEN: Yes you do. You could if you wanted.

TASH: Could I? How do you do it? You know I watch people on tubes and in the street, couples together, and I think how do they do it… Ring each other, keep seeing each other, keep wanting to be together, eat enough meals, and share enough Christmases to justify that they are no longer single.

HEN: You're too –

TASH: Don't say choosy. People always say choosy when what they really think is –

HEN: Perhaps they didn't browse long enough?

TASH: I like Al.

HEN: I like Al.

TASH: *Like?*

HEN: I *love* Al.

(*They drink.*)

This woman was in work today. Typical case. Husband had just walked out, nearly a year ago now. Paid up the mortgage, fed the cat, dry-cleaned his suit, saw she was alright, discussed with her what he'd like for his tea, left the house and just didn't bother coming back. Maybe that's what happens. Maybe you just pick something up, wear it for a while and then put it down. For most of us death or some other woman gets there before that decision is made but for some people…

TASH: You never know someone. You think you do but one day you look up and – I'm just not romantic.

HEN: Yes you are. You could have whoever you want.

TASH: Yeah, yeah, yeah… The pick up is the easy part. It's the staying with, I can't get a taste for.

HEN: What's his name?

TASH: The service is shite here.

HEN: Don't tell me...you didn't even get his name... Tash...

TASH: Squeal... His name's Squeal.

HEN: As in pig?

TASH: Yeah.

HEN: Sounds good.

TASH: Sounds nothing.

HEN: You just don't trust men.

TASH: Please. Cliché.

(*Silence.*)

I'm sorry it's just – children aren't everything.

(*Silence.*)

You alright?

HEN: (*Beat.*) Laughing.

TASH: (*Long beat.*) Do you know there are oceans of water between the stars and the moon?

## SCENE 4

*Outdoor pool. London. GLORIA sitting on the side of a swimming pool, in costume, goggles and hat as SQUEAL stands in trunks, drying himself with a towel. GLORIA suddenly flinches.*

GLORIA: Christ.

SQUEAL: Are you okay?

GLORIA: I've been... (*She cranes around, trying to see over her shoulder, feeling her back.*) ...stung.

SQUEAL: It's the start of the lazy wasps. They get lazy waking up –

GLORIA: And I'm dinner. Oow.

SQUEAL: You need vinegar.

GLORIA: Serves me right for just sitting.

(*SQUEAL makes to go.*)

You're a very good swimmer.

SQUEAL: It's a bit cold today to be honest.

GLORIA: I used to come here as a girl.

SQUEAL: Yeah?

GLORIA: Hasn't been decorated since. They're all very
    colourful here aren't they? All the people.

SQUEAL: I guess.

GLORIA: It's my daily ritual. I sit here.

SQUEAL: You don't swim…

GLORIA: Not really… If it's hot I might have a dip but…
    I just enjoy the sunshine and the people. You get to
    remembering faces.

SQUEAL: Uh huh.

GLORIA: (*Beat.*) That's how I remember yours.
    (*SQUEAL nods, smiles, turns to go.*)
    You're a lawyer.

SQUEAL: Sorry?

GLORIA: In the city. You look like a lawyer.

SQUEAL: No –

GLORIA: I sometimes get it wrong. I sit and try and work out
    what people do.
    (*GLORIA rubs her shoulder.*)

SQUEAL: It'll pass soon.

GLORIA: Little buggers.
    (*SQUEAL nods, makes to go.*)
    Teaching then?

SQUEAL: Doctor.

GLORIA: Of course. You've got the hands of a doctor.

SQUEAL: People always say –

GLORIA: It's true.

SQUEAL: People always say that.

GLORIA: My husband has the hands of a dry cleaner.
    They're soft but very red from all the fluid –

SQUEAL: He should wear –

GLORIA: I tell him.

SQUEAL: He should wear gloves. You tell him.

GLORIA: Doctor's orders. He says it keeps them soft. For
    wetting the ring of pint glasses. He wets them and rings
    them… He always knows it makes me laugh.

SQUEAL: (*Beat.*) Still –

GLORIA: Still –
    (*SQUEAL makes to go.*)

What kind of doctor?

SQUEAL: Casualty. I'm a houseman. I'm just in casualty at the moment.

GLORIA: But you're helping people. That means something.

SQUEAL: Yeah, sewing up knife wounds and mopping up drunks.

GLORIA: Your family must be very –

SQUEAL: Just my dad. Yeah, he thinks it's alright.

GLORIA: He must be very proud. A doctor.

SQUEAL: No –

GLORIA: A doctor is what every one wants in the family.

SQUEAL: He doesn't say much. I never know.

GLORIA: He will be.

SQUEAL: You think? (*Beat.*) He has a bad heart.

GLORIA: That's no excuse. Make sure he tells you.

SQUEAL: Okay…

GLORIA: Gloria.

SQUEAL: I'll tell him, Gloria.

GLORIA: You tell him. People don't appreciate each other enough.

(*Silence. SQUEAL picks up his wet towel, turns to go.*)

SQUEAL: You should have a swim. It's great once you get in.

GLORIA: Too chilly for me today…

SQUEAL: You always just sit?

GLORIA: You been watching me?

SQUEAL: It's a waste of a ticket.

GLORIA: Giving me the eye.

SQUEAL: It must be a couple of quid a day. You'd be as good sitting by the pond than…

GLORIA: (*Sharp.*) It's company.

(*Silence. SQUEAL hovers.*)

Sometimes conversation. I fall into conversation. I met a woman last week who'd lost an eye.

SQUEAL: That was careless.

GLORIA: Cricket bat in the eye. She said it gave her a whole different perspective.

SQUEAL: It would.

GLORIA: Losing an eye like that. (*Beat.*) You probably see
that all the time.

SQUEAL: It's still a shock.

GLORIA: Yeah.

SQUEAL: Still would take some getting used to.

GLORIA: Yeah. (*Beat.*) How would you put your mascara on?
(*A half ripple of laughter. SQUEAL hovers.*)

SQUEAL: Right... Okay... Vinegar on that wasp sting.

GLORIA: I can't even feel it.

SQUEAL: Bye then...
(*As SQUEAL turns to go.*)

GLORIA: I can't swim... I can doggy paddle a bit but –

SQUEAL: That's a start.

GLORIA: Marvin was fantastic swimmer. I wonder now why
I never... I just sit at the side.

SQUEAL: You should give it a go.

GLORIA: I don't like to get my ears wet.

SQUEAL: They do classes.

GLORIA: I'd hold everyone back.

SQUEAL: I saw a big man must have been about eighteen
stone and he was learning the other week...

GLORIA: I'd be their first drowning.

SQUEAL: You'd float.

GLORIA: Not me. I'd sink to the bottom.

SQUEAL: No you wouldn't.

GLORIA: How do you know?

SQUEAL: Well whatever.

GLORIA: Yeah whatever.

SQUEAL: Breast stroke's easy.

GLORIA: I'm sure...

SQUEAL: Dead easy... I could...

GLORIA: What?
(*SQUEAL hovers.*)

SQUEAL: I better get off. Careful you don't roast. Your
shoulders look...

GLORIA: Yes...

SQUEAL: They're's nothing to be frightened of. Lifeguards all
round the edge and people everywhere to save you.

GLORIA: (*Almost to herself.*) A doctor.

SQUEAL: Bye, Gloria.

(*SQUEAL makes to go.*)

GLORIA: He should look at you and say I'm proud you're my son.

SQUEAL: Squeal.

GLORIA: The runt of the litter.

SQUEAL: Yeah. (*He hesitates and turns back.*) Gloria...

GLORIA: Yeah.

SQUEAL: If you want...

GLORIA: Yes.

SQUEAL: If you'd let me...

GLORIA: Please.

SQUEAL: Breast stroke's the easiest one to get.

(*GLORIA turns, smiles. Holds his stare. Too long. She tentatively nods her head.*)

## SCENE 5

*Supermarket, South London. AL is wheeling a shopping trolley. HEN is ahead, contemplating the cereals.*

HEN: So you never wonder?

AL: Nah?

HEN: You never imagine for one moment what it might have been like if it had been someone else?

AL: It wasn't. It was you.

HEN: So you think it's fate.

AL: It's choice. You have a choice as to how you live your life. Some are good at it, some are crap.

HEN: So you chose me.

AL: Not exactly. There are random moments and moments of decision. You were a moment of decision following a random event.

HEN: We've been together for the last six years. What's random about that?

AL: It wasn't planned. Getting pregnant was a random event.

HEN: And you think that's what makes up life?

AL: We came to buy some cereal. You said you were hungry
and it had to be cereal.

HEN: We were drunk.

AL: Random moment.

HEN: Choice to keep it?

AL: Moment of decision.

HEN: And you think that's what makes up life?

AL: I don't know. I'm a builder.

HEN: So.

AL: We got peanut butter?

HEN: It's a lifetime. We are talking about a lifetime.

AL: Have you been talking to Tash again?

HEN: I always talk to Tash.

AL: She's single –

HEN: So.

AL: And thirty –

HEN: Just. And that makes her bitter?

AL: It makes her stir it with her mates who have people.

HEN: You don't have me.

AL: Cheers.

HEN: Don't you ever think you have me.

AL: Alright...alright... Keep your wig on.

HEN: Sometimes you make me nervous.

AL: Right.

HEN: You can react a bit.

AL: Alright. (*Beat.*) Right.

HEN: Is that it?

AL: Hen, where you from?

HEN: Southall.

AL: Where am I from?

HEN: Southall.

AL: So what does that say?

HEN: What?

AL: What does that say?

HEN: We both know where to go to get a good curry?

AL: It says you know me. And I know you. And your dad
knows where I live so if I did anything to make you
nervous he doesn't have to walk far to do me one.

HEN: 'Til death us do part?

(*AL avoids this conversation concentrating on the cereal choice.*)

AL: Crunchy? (*Holding up jar.*) I'm getting crunchy.

HEN: A baby's a lifetime.

AL: Only swans mate for life.

HEN: You're cynical.

AL: Couldn't even spell it. I'm not cynical, I'm pulling your leg. I said yes. I said yes, didn't I?

HEN: This isn't just you and me. It isn't like a quickie and a phone number scribbled down on the back of your hand.

AL: It's hardly a teen cock up. We've been going six years, Hen.

HEN: I don't want to end up like Tash. I don't want to wake up and find myself on my own with a kid.

AL: She hasn't got one.

HEN: But she's on her own.

AL: There are worse things.

HEN: What are you saying?

AL: People do it. Bring up kids on their own.

HEN: Is that what you're suggesting?

AL: No. No.

HEN: You're winding me up now.

AL: We're having a baby.

HEN: And that's alright with you?

AL: I said yes.

HEN: But you've hardly thought about it.

AL: What's there to think about?

HEN: Like where we're going to live, if I'm going to give up my job, whose name he's going to have.

AL: So we've decided it's a boy then.

HEN: It's not funny. Like if you want it.

AL: Yeah, I want it.

HEN: You wouldn't have wanted to wait?

AL: Maybe a year or so but –

HEN: See –

AL: But only 'til the house was finished. I wanted us to be able to live in the house.

HEN: What are you saying? What are you saying?

AL: I'm saying if we were working to Railtrack Guidelines
then maybe we might have kicked around waiting a bit
longer but... Hen... We only came out to buy cereal.

HEN: Do you love me?

AL: They've got an offer on Pampers.

HEN: Do you love me?

AL: (*Beat.*) With all my heart. (*He moves off with the trolley.*) I'll
get this.

HEN: (*Beat.*) I don't want to be like Tash. I don't want to be
like Tash living in a shit heap, no one to love, moving from
one naff job to another –

AL: Maybe she finds happiness in other ways.

## SCENE 6

*Loft apartment, Soho, London. NATHAN is sitting in his loft apartment;
modernist, Conranesque, slick in Joseph sweats, dressing gown and Nike.
He butters a bagel. TASH stands videoing him.*

TASH: And what exactly are you doing now?

NATHAN: I'm buttering a bagel. Then...depending on my
mood, I will place a small square leaf of smoked salmon
on the top, sometimes I might slice a pickle but mostly, it's
a nub of black pepper and my dark coffee which I get at
Grodinski's, the FT if I feel in the mood.

TASH: And you always put the salmon on after?

NATHAN: The bagel, then the cheese, then the salmon, then
the pepper.

TASH: Or the pickle.

NATHAN: The pickle if I'm in the mood or even a lemon.

TASH: Now what would I do?

NATHAN: Well you could say something like – 'Would you
find it useful if perhaps, you could buy it all in one pack,
cheese, bagel, salmon, pepper...?'

TASH: Lemon?

NATHAN: And the lemon. Say in one pack?

TASH: You want me to kind of think along those sort of lines?

NATHAN: The company is paid to see where the gap is in the
market. To see the way people live, eat, consume. So if you

can come up with any observations along the way, that's
great. That's dandy.

TASH: Okay...

NATHAN: I hope you don't mind this. Doing this meeting in
my flat? It's just Sundays –

TASH: Sundays. I know Sundays are sacred.

NATHAN: Most of my employees hot desk anyway. We're
rarely ever in the same room at the same time. Tash.
Natasha. Russian?

TASH: Croydon.

NATHAN: Try and hold the camera level if you can. It's just
the clients get pissed off –

TASH: Sure –

NATHAN: Fuck it. I'm the boss. You wobble if you like.
(*Beat.*) So?

TASH: So... Would you find it useful if perhaps you could buy
it all in one pack, cheese, bagel, salmon, pepper, lemon?

NATHAN: It's an idea. Maybe a gimmick but I can do it
myself. The enjoyment is doing it yourself. They might
say something like that. You often find people initiate the
opposite response if you present them with a specific idea.
Remember to get them to hold up the packet of whatever
they're buying to the camera. We need to show the client,
to let them see their branding.

TASH: Okay... Could you hold up the lid of the cheese
packet? I've just got to logo register.
(*NATHAN holds up the lid for the camera. TASH films it
zooming in.*)
We're very grateful.

NATHAN: I'm happy to oblige.

TASH: We're finding logos very important at the moment.
Red's always a good colour. See a red logo on the cheese
lid. It's probably what made you buy it.

NATHAN: That's great. That shows initiative, it's just a little
more than you need.

TASH: Right, sorry.

NATHAN: I think you're great at this, Tash. You're spot on.

TASH: Yeah?

NATHAN: Really...really great.

> (*NATHAN reads his paper, aware he is being filmed. He pours himself another cup of coffee, adding sugar, then pouring in a little more coffee.*)

TASH: Coffee...then sugar...then coffee?

NATHAN: It melts it quicker. It's a habit. Nothing else.

TASH: It's interesting.

> (*NATHAN pours another cup and places it opposite him.*)
> And you're pouring another cup?

NATHAN: For you.

TASH: Thanks.

> (*NATHAN flicks through a CV as he eats and drinks.*)

NATHAN: You've done a lot of jobs. Your CV shows a lot of jobs.

TASH: Yeah.

> (*NATHAN is buttering a second bagel and placing it on a plate opposite.*)

NATHAN: Eat.

> (*TASH puts down the camera.*)

TASH: Cheers.

NATHAN: There's no harm in that. Taking your time to find what you really want to do.

TASH: Would I be doing this in people's houses?

NATHAN: Sometimes but... Mainly supermarkets, the large food chains. I go out and do it myself sometimes. That's unusual in the agency but I like to keep in touch. It makes the client feel like I really know their product.
> (*Silence.*)
> I spend a lot of time with housewives. They tend to be our biggest resource. I think you'll be good with them. (*Beat.*) It's quick money.

TASH: That's what I always want. I've been doing up a flat... Talking about doing up my flat. (*Beat.*) I never do. (*Beat.*) Earning money...earning money can be a motivation. (*She sniffs the coffee.*) Real.
> (*NATHAN shrugs.*)
> You don't look like an instant man.

(*TASH rests her camera on the side and sits down to take the coffee.*)

NATHAN: Good. Good observational skills –

(*Silence. NATHAN pours her another cup of coffee. TASH smiles, a little embarrassed. NATHAN smiles a little embarrassed.*)

TASH: You live on your own? It feels as if…

(*Silence.*)

NATHAN: (*Beat.*) It takes getting used to, living on your own. So you're interested?

TASH: Yeah…

NATHAN: Good…that's great. Well, let's get you rocking and rolling. How about starting –

TASH: Today. I could start today.

NATHAN: Tomorrow's fine just I'll walk you down just…let me take a shower.

(*TASH nods, flicking the camera up.*)

TASH: Of course. We want you just to do everything as you would normally do.

(*NATHAN gets up to shower.*)

NATHAN: You can put down the camera now.

TASH: I was just getting into it.

(*NATHAN eats a tangerine. TASH flicks the camera back on him.*)

(*Beat.*) Fruit. You always end with fruit?

(*NATHAN holds up the tangerine bag label up to the camera; smiling.*)

NATHAN: It aids digestion. See, I logo registered, Natasha.

TASH: …you do seem to have picked up the technique, Nathan.

(*NATHAN eats. TASH sits, stealing a bagel from his plate.*)

I'll walk you down.

# SCENE 7

*A park, South London. GLORIA is sitting on a park bench with SQUEAL. They are eating sandwiches and take-away drinks enjoying the sunshine. Their hair is wet. They've just been for a swim.*

SQUEAL: You breathe out as you pull.

GLORIA: I drown if I breathe and I pull. I open my mouth and I drown.

SQUEAL: So you close your mouth, then you breath out through your nose.

GLORIA: That's unhealthy. That's bad for you. In through your nose, out through your mouth. Germs pass that way.

SQUEAL: You're swimming in a thousand gallons of chlorine, anything would be zapped. (*Beat.*) You're funny. You're pulling my leg.

(*GLORIA laughs to herself.*)

GLORIA: Gullible.

SQUEAL: Not in the dictionary.

GLORIA: It's so nice with the sun.

SQUEAL: Yes.

GLORIA: I feel so nice. (*Beat.*) I walked past your flat the other day.

SQUEAL: Yeah…

GLORIA: The one with the bins outside.

SQUEAL: It's good for the hospital.

GLORIA: I couldn't live without my garden.

SQUEAL: Gloria –

GLORIA: I did live with my husband but he's not there anymore.

SQUEAL: You still wear your wedding ring?

GLORIA: Can't get it off.

SQUEAL: My dad still wears his.

(*Silence.*)

A garden must be great in this weather.

GLORIA: It is now. Was a state but… I've almost finished it now. Patio and a little pond near the shed. With fish. I wanted Koi carp but they're expensive. £200. Imagine paying that for a bag of fish and chips? (*Beat.*) Frogs and goldfish are just as nice. (*Beat.*) He liked fish and chips.

SQUEAL: You never had –

GLORIA: No. Marvin was always handful enough... I was never the mothering kind.

(*GLORIA watches something in the distance.*)

There are girls who take men down here and do things behind those trees, aren't there? I'm not stupid. If you sit here long enough. (*Beat.*) Good job it's summer. Maybe that's what my husband did. Maybe he used to come down here and pick up a girl and stand up against a tree and... They would have sex. And maybe one day he couldn't come back and face me with it. Maybe he knew I'd smell it on him or just know. A wife's instinct.

SQUEAL: I don't think...

GLORIA: You didn't know him. Maybe that's what he did. And maybe afterwards she would hand him her knickers and fold them into a little square and let him slip them in his pocket. And maybe he would come home and for his tea, and sit down and eat whatever I've put in front of him and all the time he'd be thinking I've got some girl's pants in my pocket. (*Beat.*) Could you never see yourself doing that if you were married?

SQUEAL: No, Gloria.

GLORIA: You say that.

SQUEAL: No.

GLORIA: Just a thought. There's a bench as well. By the pond. And John next door is going to help me build a Gazebo.

SQUEAL: Is that edible?

GLORIA: For flowers. For sitting. For sitting in and thinking. He won't recognise the place when he gets back, will he Squeal?

SQUEAL: I don't know.

GLORIA: That man...

(*GLORIA has not taken her eyes off someone in the distance.*)

...with the cap on... That man. Can you see that man? Go over. Will you... Just... Squeal... Will you... He's wearing... That cap... Like my... Please will you just look for me... Just go over and ask him...

SQUEAL: I don't know him, Gloria. I never...

GLORIA: (*With realisation.*) It's not him. (*Beat.*) It's alright. It's not him.

SQUEAL: I'm sorry.

GLORIA: I drive everyone mad. I always think...

> (*SQUEAL puts out his hand and rests it on GLORIA's. She tentatively tightens her grip around it, stroking it.*)

I'm always wrong...

SQUEAL: Gloria...

GLORIA: Have you ever been in love?

SQUEAL: Gloria...

GLORIA: I don't mean married love. I mean love with no responsibility. Love with no expectation. Love without the cleaning and the washing shirts.

SQUEAL: Sometimes...

> (*GLORIA loosens her grip on his hand.*)

GLORIA: Yes.

SQUEAL: (*Beat.*) Maybe sometimes I think I could be... I could fall...become in love with someone.

GLORIA: And her?

SQUEAL: (*Beat.*) She's a bit slower on the uptake.

> (*A long silence as GLORIA sits clearly upset, clearly not willing to speak.*)

You should try backstroke. Backstroke's the easiest. Next week I'll show you backstroke.

> (*GLORIA turns and looks at him. She nods. She smiles.*)

GLORIA: And after I could cook your tea.

> (*SQUEAL does not know what to say.*)

SQUEAL: If you want.

GLORIA: I bet you like...

SQUEAL: Everything.

> (*The squawk of birds as SQUEAL and GLORIA both instinctively look up. The slow beat of wings as if in a flock on migration.*)

GLORIA: I wonder where they're going to.

# SCENE 8

*Bar, Soho, London. TASH and HEN. Same bar. Same drinks. Same routine. Loud.*

TASH: So I'm sitting there thinking this is weird, I'm sitting there seriously wondering how I'm going to get myself out of this one because I don't know if you remember but when I lived with Itkin.

HEN: The Jewish boy from hell.

TASH: I was writing the name in all the mirrors if you remember and something which I, now, as a reformed character...

HEN: Since the pickled cow incident.

TASH: Since I spilt my emotional innards out all over the carpet of that coke trodden single cracked orchid shit hole in the heart of metropolis, do not and for full velocity of that concept, do not let grace my nostrils or gums. I am not looking to get drawn into flagrante delicto with some twisted sister, battered childhood, anal retentive and other sexual deviant practising tosser, even if he does have a white peace pad in Soho. I am not looking for a shag with an emotional timebomb just waiting to explode all over my life, probably into my bank account and certainly an experience which will entail several short sharp trips to the Woman's centre, your legs up in stirrups trying to deny any knowledge of that large scaly pustule adorning your feminine minge.

HEN: You slept with him.

TASH: Excuse me. I don't spend all day listening to the rejected. He was nice... He walked me down... It's going well. The job. I'm not interested... I'm really not interested. He's obviously the kind of guy who gets dumped.

HEN: When did you get so bitter, Tash?

TASH: Sorry?

HEN: You slept with him.

*(AL walks in.)*

TASH: Alright. You coming to the –

HEN: Sorry I meant to –

TASH: No that's fine, that's great…

>    (*AL kisses HEN hello as he gestures to the waiter for a drink.*
>    *TASH kisses AL.*)

AL: Alright Tash.

TASH: Hello gorgeous.

AL: What time's the – ?

HEN: Eight.

TASH: (*To AL.*) You won't like it. It's that thing with –

HEN: The girl who's in –

TASH: It's romantic…

HEN: Playing the monkey?

TASH: She wasn't a monkey.

HEN: They were all bloody monkeys. She was in love with –

AL: I like romantic films.

TASH: Great.

>    (*Silence.*)

>    How's the house?

AL: Put the windows in at the weekend.

HEN: Sash. They're reclaimed sash.

TASH: Nice one. I've not even stripped a wall yet.

HEN: Al could –

AL: Yeah, I could –

TASH: No, I'm alright –

HEN: We've got a steamer.

AL: It's like butter with a steamer.

TASH: I like the walls.

HEN: They're bloody awful.

TASH: They're *my* bloody awful. (*Beat.*) I like them. Cheers
    but –

AL: You're fine.

HEN: Sorry I should have –

TASH: It's fine. I guess we got the –

AL: Booby prize.

TASH: …night your mates didn't need you to sit on their sofas
    like lard, drink beer and watch football.

HEN: Nasty. Why are you two so nasty to each other?

TASH: We are lovely to each other.

AL: I didn't say a word.

HEN: We should –
TASH: We're fine.
HEN: The trailers. Al likes to watch the trailers.
AL: That's not true. It's fine.
HEN: Three's a very bad number. Three is notoriously difficult. Someone is always left out.
TASH: Which book are you reading now?
HEN: It's not a book. I'm just saying.
TASH: How do you live with her?
AL: Take the pills and buy in Sky Sport.
TASH: You're looking very toned.
AL: I've been working a lot –
TASH: So are you going to let this one finally stop and give herself a rest?
HEN: We can go and see a film together. We can go and see a bloody film together.
TASH: You didn't mention he was coming.
HEN: It was last minute.
TASH: You should have said if you wanted to spend the evening with Al.
HEN: I wanted to spend an evening with you both. This isn't a competition.
TASH: What you talking about? (*To AL.*) Do you know what she is talking about?
HEN: You don't help yourself Tash. You don't make yourself easy.
TASH: What? I don't discuss window frames and what colour carpets and what wallpaper I need to put up on my walls and –
HEN: I don't mean that. You make it hard for people to like you.
(*Silence. TASH laughs. HEN laughs.*)
It's a bloody film. We can go and see a bloody film without it turning into full combat.
AL: Sorry.
TASH: You don't have to be sorry.
AL: I wasn't talking to you.
HEN: Al.
(*Silence.*)

Get over it you two, eh?

TASH: You want to do my decorating?

AL: If you like. With the steamer I've got, I tell you it's like cutting through –

TASH: Yeah. Okay. Thanks.

(*TASH thinks of offering some gesture of affection; instead she chinks her glass with HEN, leans forward and kisses AL on the cheek.*)

AL: Hen says you've got a new job.

HEN: Market research.

AL: That's probably good money.

TASH: It's sitting looking at people's sad lives.

AL: I guess it depends how you're feeling. Everyone looks sad if you're feeling –

TASH: A bit blue? Don't say a bit blue. (*Looking to AL.*) I saw you the other week.

AL: Yeah?

TASH: Lunch hour. You were with –

AL: My boss' daughter's doing work placement.

HEN: What's her name? She's got a lovely name.

AL: If it's a girl, we're going to call her Natasha.

(*AL holds TASH's stare.*)

Like butter. I'll come over next week.

TASH: Great.

HEN: (*Beat.*) He hasn't done the job yet.

(*HEN breaks into a smile, pushing him affectionately as a ripple of laughter finally breaks between the three. HEN wets her finger and absently rings the top of her glass. It makes a low long hum.*)

## SCENE 9

*Street, London. TASH in a hurry, dressed up. Rain. Traffic. SQUEAL running past showering under a wadge of documents, in a hurry, not slowing down.*

TASH: So I was thinking –

SQUEAL: Sorry?

TASH: These oceans. Do they have fish in? Do they have
    whales and if that is the case, that is officially a mammal
    and where there are mammals there are humans, so are
    therefore the stars planets, with people living on them and
    those oceans of water are like our Atlantic?
SQUEAL: I don't know what you're –
TASH: I knew you were a bullshitter –
SQUEAL: Sorry.
TASH: If you were telling the truth, you would be pleased
    that I have remembered your late night ramblings and be
    willing to defend your theory –
SQUEAL: It's raining –
TASH: This precludes thought.
SQUEAL: (*Beat.*) Hello Tash –
TASH: I'm passed that bit. I'm mid-sentence with you now –
SQUEAL: I'm on call.
TASH: Yeah, me too. Consultancy, it's the direction most
    people in marketing are going now –
SQUEAL: What?
TASH: So your theory is flunked.
SQUEAL: Right.
TASH: Doesn't matter.
SQUEAL: We're getting –
TASH: I hate umbrellas. I think people who carry umbrellas
    look too –
SQUEAL: Prepared.
TASH: – anal. I find that a big turn off.
SQUEAL: I don't carry one. Do you?
TASH: Do you? Sorry. You go.
SQUEAL: Coffee. Do you want a get a coffee?
TASH: No.
SQUEAL: Okay.
TASH: I'm –
SQUEAL: Sure. Definitely.
TASH: Decorating. Got a mate decorating. A mate's bloke.
    She's pregnant. Very nearly due.
SQUEAL: Great.
TASH: They were planning but they weren't planning then
    bam –

SQUEAL: It's not as hard as it looks.

TASH: No. (*Going.*) I'm decorating. I've got a mate decorating. My mate's bloke. He's –

SQUEAL: Great.

TASH: That's your favourite word.

SQUEAL: A man of few.

TASH: Okay then. Bye.

(*TASH makes to go.*)

SQUEAL: Is that it? 'Okay then. Bye.'

TASH: I'm going for mauve on the kitchen walls and yellow in the bedroom. I know purple's a bit ecclesiastical but fuck it, it's a nice colour, it's a calming colour.

SQUEAL: What are you talking about Tash?

TASH: I thought you wanted to talk a bit longer.

SQUEAL: Why are you so weird? Why can't you just do simple things normal?

TASH: I'm talking.

SQUEAL: You're being all weird.

TASH: Weird like what?

SQUEAL: Weird like this. I only asked you for a cup of coffee. It's okay, you don't have to say yes. I'm not breaking my heart over it.

TASH: Fine. Okay. Nice seeing you then.

SQUEAL: Tash.

TASH: Do you know that a woman was standing on a golf course in Berkshire and it was raining so hard that a small koi carp with an ID tag clipped on its fin fell from the sky? It had got vacummed up in the big weather cycle in Tokyo. I read that in the paper this morning.

SQUEAL: (*Laughing.*) You're amazing.

TASH: At least I'm making conversation. I'm talking, saying something instead of 'Yeah great'.

SQUEAL: Okay.

TASH: It's hardly fighting the chemistry. You could hardly say that you and I talk and we're fighting the chemistry.

SQUEAL: Slow down, slow down.

TASH: You get good value for money with me.

SQUEAL: I never said –

TASH: If you want to talk to one of those daft bitches who
simper at your every word, then go fling around your
'greats' and 'yeah okay' somewhere else.

SQUEAL: Fine, cheers, enough said. Have a nice day.

TASH: Don't look injured.

SQUEAL: Look what?

TASH: If you can't do it, don't stop me in the street and say
hello. I've passed you twice this week –

SQUEAL: I didn't see you –

TASH: – on the bus and you've said fuck all.

(*Silence.*)

SQUEAL: On the bus?

(*Silence. TASH and SQUEAL start to laugh.*)

How was I meant to see you if you were sitting on a bloody
bus?

(*Silence.*)

TASH: Goodbye then.

SQUEAL: We could go and have a coffee.

TASH: No thanks.

SQUEAL: (*Calling after.*) Tash... Tash... Can I have your
phone number?

TASH: What? And never fucking call?

(*TASH exits. SQUEAL looks on. Rain.*)

## SCENE 10

*Flat, London. AL scraping paper off the walls with long smooth moves.
TASH standing, eating back of the fridge food.*

AL: China and Malaysia. There's a few left in India, but to be
honest the indigenous Tiger, I reckon there's probably not
more than 100 – 150 left in the world.

TASH: Right.

AL: That doesn't include breeds in captivity. There's a small
ratio of the rarer breeds that are surviving solely on the fact
that there are a quantity of them still bred in captivity. Like
the Siberian White Tiger which I reckon there aren't more
than 30 – 35 alive in the wild.

TASH: Yeah.

AL: Remember I adopted one for Hen's brother last
Christmas. Whipsnade do them.

TASH: Yeah. I remember her saying.

AL: You'll get indigestion eating like that.

TASH: It's the way I always eat.

AL: If you folded out that table you could move my brushes
over a bit and sit down.

TASH: I like standing up. I'm going out later.

AL: My dad got a hernia always eating standing up on the job
– Conductor.

TASH: Yeah, Al. I know. You say it everytime you come
around and I'm standing eating like this.

AL: Mind my own. Sorry. These are good walls underneath
here.

TASH: Yeah, what's Hen doing tonight?

AL: Watching telly. I'll get us a takeaway later.

TASH: Friday night and you're staying in?

AL: Yeah.

TASH: Friday night and you're staying in?

AL: We got a parrot in here? We can't do much at the
moment. Hen's knackered.

TASH: She shouldn't be working.

AL: I keep telling her.

TASH: Do you?

AL: Yeah. What you looking at me like that for?

TASH: How long have you been with Hen?

AL: '94, '95 – Six years.

TASH: Long time.

AL: Life time. For me. I couldn't get a girlfriend before her.

TASH: Really?

AL: Ha ha. (*Pointing to ceiling.*) You want me to do that bit as
well?

(*TASH nods.*)

Hen keeps saying, when are you going to settle?

TASH: No. You all have a perverse interest in understanding
why I'm not doing what you're all doing. I think you're
worried I know something you don't. I don't mind. My
family have long stopped minding. This is it. This is me.

AL: Nice cornicing.

TASH: I love you.

AL: I don't make her work. I'd prefer it if she didn't work.

TASH: You need the money, she says.

AL: We'd manage.

TASH: Doing up your house is like haemorrhaging money.

AL: It's a good investment.

TASH: You've been stung.

AL: Bollocks, you don't know what you're talking about.

TASH: I saw you.

AL: What? I can scrape off the paint around the moulding that will clean it up a bit.

TASH: I saw you. How old is she? Sixteen? Seventeen?

AL: I don't know what you're talking about.

TASH: Boss' daughter? Work placement?

AL: (*Laughing.*) You can't be serious. I'm not taking it serious. You are being serious. How long have I been with Hen? How long have you known me?

TASH: You're still a bloke.

(*AL stops work, laughing.*)

AL: You're serious.

(*TASH makes to go.*)

TASH: You're insulted.

AL: Too fucking right I'm insulted. A sixteen year old temp. Not finished her A levels. You don't get it do you? You sad, silly cow, you don't get it.

TASH: I'm just saying. I know. I'm just saying I know. So do something about it.

AL: (*Beat.*) What were we doing? On this hot date? What were we doing?

TASH: You were buying sandwiches. You were having a sandwich.

AL: Bloody hell. Ham or egg?

TASH: Don't piss around.

AL: You don't piss around. You don't fucking piss around. Tash. Are you honestly serious?

TASH: You touched her arm. You were holding her by the arm. Sort it out or I'm telling Hen.

AL: Telling her what? (*Beat.*) Telling her what?

TASH: Don't make me say it.

AL: You don't know what you're fucking talking about.
(*Silence.*)
When was the last time you were touched eh? Can you
remember? And I don't mean some drunk grope in the
back of a cab. When was the last time? I'll tell you when
I was. This morning, just as I was going out, I reached for
my keys and Hen brushed the back of my neck. She leant
back, from reading her visa bill and she stroked the back
of my neck. I've had six years of that and I still like it. And
you think I'd give that up for some tossy little feel over a
mozzarella and avocado ciabatta.
(*Silence.*)
You should get out more.

TASH: (*Beat.*) Too much keeping me up at night.

AL: Like you're proud of it. Like picking men up in the way
you do is something to brag about...

TASH: I hinted. There was no bragging involved.

AL: So why tell Hen all about it all the time? (*Beat.*) It hurts
her.

TASH: Maybe I'm having a better time.

AL: She loves you.
(*TASH holds AL's stare.*)

TASH: You haven't got the monopoly on that. (*Beat.*) Do
something.

AL: Six years? You think I'm about to throw away six years?
(*AL returns to scraping the walls. TASH carries on eating,
watching him.*)
I don't know what you're talking about.

# SCENE 11

*Supermarket, South London. SQUEAL is standing talking to NATHAN
who is videoing him as he takes things off shelves and puts them into
his basket.*

NATHAN: And coffee is how you start your day?

SQUEAL: Yeah. I suppose so. Yeah, coffee is what I normally
have. Does the shop pay you to do this?

NATHAN: It's client based. If you could just turn the lid a little, so I could catch the label. Logo registering.

SQUEAL: I don't really believe in this.

NATHAN: It's helping people. It's helping us help people decide what they need to buy.

SQUEAL: What they *need* to buy? What you want them to buy?

NATHAN: And after the coffee?

SQUEAL: I'm sure you have to do your job but I've just come in for a jar of coffee maybe some biscuits for later not to help your fat cat boss shove us more junk we don't need, okay?

NATHAN: Yeah, I completely understand it's just your input would be invaluable. I just have two more people to do and then I can finish for the day.

SQUEAL: It's only half past eight.

NATHAN: I started early. I was let down.

SQUEAL: And I do night shifts so if you wouldn't mind.
(*A man, MARVIN, shuffles past, a pint of milk in hand, browsing over tea bags. SQUEAL resumes his search for the biscuits.*)

NATHAN: (*To MARVIN.*) This is the tea and coffee section, don't let me disturb your normal pattern of behaviour but was that actually the teabags you were looking for?

MARVIN: It's whatever's the cheapest.

NATHAN: Interesting. Very interesting. You work?

MARVIN: Sorry.

NATHAN: You do something in the service industry.

MARVIN: Sorry.

NATHAN: We find a high percentage of the technical professions or even service industry tend to favour that brand of particular beverage.

SQUEAL: The guy is just buying tea. Could you not go and do this somewhere else?

NATHAN: You see I'd like to be able to say yes but this is highly important, highly sensitive information.

MARVIN: I work in the cleaning industry. I like to bring my own tea.

NATHAN: Right. So I wasn't that far left of field. Very
  interesting. Very kind of you to divulge. Share.
  (*SQUEAL shakes his head as he makes to go.*)
  You will be having milk with that coffee?
SQUEAL: Possibly.
NATHAN: Natural or freeze dried? (*Beat.*) Coffee mate or
  cow's own?
SQUEAL: Are you taking the piss?
MARVIN: Excuse me, do you know where they've moved the
  detergents?
SQUEAL: Sorry?
  (*MARVIN moves off. SQUEAL continues with his shopping.*
  *NATHAN films throughout.*)
  Could you stop that now please? Please? (*To checkout girl.*)
  Could you tell him to stop or I'll call the manager? Please.
  It's been a long night. I've been on the night shift. Please.
  (*NATHAN refuses to stop as he films the contents of the*
  *shopping bag.*)
NATHAN: Almost finished.
MARVIN: I think you should perhaps leave the gentleman
  alone.
NATHAN: It's important for the advertising...
SQUEAL: You should know better. You should know better
  not to tell people to drink more, to eat more, to live more,
  to buy more. Do you know what people like you do?
  The damage that people like you do. I see the damage
  that people like you create. The stress in people's lives to
  buy more, to keep up the mortgage repayments, to have
  another drink to eleviate that stress, to eat another fat
  filled pile of crap which clogs up the heart and makes it
  difficult to live, to even breathe. I've just spent last night
  working on the heart of a very fat man, opening it up and
  discovering the consequences of what you sell. The pain
  that you deliver. The hope that you give people, to make
  their lives better, for more, more, more.
  (*SQUEAL, through his tirade, has managed to push the man*
  *up against the wall of the supermarket as MARVIN looks on.*)

What happened to love and care and not thinking that
*you* know what people *need?* When they don't even know
themselves.

MARVIN: Alright, son. Calm down? Okay?

(*SQUEAL slowly eases his grip, nodding. Then holding up the
bottle of coffee he shows the label to the camera.*)

NATHAN: I'm sorry. I'm really very sorry.

(*SQUEAL turns and puts down his coffee and exits.
MARVIN takes in the scene.*)

MARVIN: You alright?

(*NATHAN nods.*)

If he'd thumped, you could have sued.

(*NATHAN nods, clearly shaken as MARVIN resumes his
shopping.*)

NATHAN: Would you mind if I filmed you doing that?

(*MARVIN shakes his head and shuffles away, with NATHAN
following him.*)

It would help if we start with your name.

MARVIN: (*Long beat.*) Marvin.

(*MARVIN turns and hesitates, staring at first NATHAN and
then the camera.*)

I know you. I clean in your block.

NATHAN: Do you?

MARVIN: I do all the blocks around there.

NATHAN: Marvin.

MARVIN: (*Beat.*) I'm looking for the polish but they've
moved it all around so – I'm lost.

NATHAN: (*Without looking up from camera.*) And now you are
found.

## INTERVAL

## SCENE 12

*Surburban garden, East London. GLORIA is hanging out washing.*
*HEN is standing talking to her. GLORIA keeps coming to a man's shirt*
*at the bottom of the pile and stopping herself, shuffling through the wet*
*washing for anything but –*

GLORIA: You don't normally. It's not normal for you to visit
  at home.
  (*Silence.*)
HEN: We had an anonymous call last week. A possible
  sighting. It's the normal feedback when we've done any
  recent press release. People want to help but this time, I
  have to say the description was surprisingly accurate.
  (*GLORIA stands frozen to the spot.*)
  It's several hundred miles from here but it could be...
GLORIA: Do you know the American backstroke is different
  from the English?
  (*HEN shakes her head. GLORIA puts down her washing and*
  *demonstrates, kicking with one arm and a leg.*)
  It's a sharp straight down movement, so you slice the
  water. I've been learning them both and it definitely
  improves your speed, not that I am concerned about speed
  but it is nice to know one has the option.
  (*HEN nods. GLORIA smiles. She takes the washing inside.*
  *HEN shifts her hand suddenly across her bump. She felt*
  *something kick.*)
HEN: I'm sure he doesn't think that.
GLORIA: How do you know?
HEN: Those who are left often blame themselves.
GLORIA: And those who leave should stop and think what
  they're bloody doing. (*Beat.*) Shouldn't they?
HEN: Do you want to follow up that sighting. It is quite a way
  away but –
GLORIA: How far?
HEN: Skye. Just off the coast of Skye.
  (*Silence.*)

I've an address. If you'll take it. Or I can arrange for
someone to perhaps go with you if you don't want to go on
your own.

(*Silence.*)

No one is forcing you.

(*Silence.*)

There's no guarantee. I don't want to raise your hopes.

GLORIA: But anything is better than nothing?

(*GLORIA pauses, looking down into the washing basket. She
is down to the last shirt.*)

I don't miss his nail clippings in the bath, coat never hung
up, channel flicking, he always was channel flicking just
when you were settling down, enjoying something. The
way he ate, he was a noisy eater, a little click, his jaw
clicked, clicked so I knew he was sat at the table before I'd
even put the plates down. I don't miss his silence and his
little observations, the birds, we've got a lot of birds in the
garden... 'Look, Gloria, isn't that a...' I don't know. I don't
know. 'The blue one, the little blue one with the yellow tip,
look it up in the book...' Always reading too late at night,
reading me bits, letting me fall asleep while he was reading
me bits. And always being too hot, always too hot in bed,
getting up to get water in the night and waking me...
'Sweetheart, have a sip. You don't drink enough.' I don't.
He's right, I don't.

HEN: If it is him?

GLORIA: You ever sit in silence with someone so long...that
only the fart behind his newspaper breaks it...makes you
laugh. The way he used to do that. Always used to do that.
All those little things.

(*Silence.*)

I guess that's married life for you.

HEN: (*Beat.*) I'm not married.

GLORIA: Who is now? Kids, and love and electric bills aren't
really that important. What's holding us together is very
fragile indeed.

HEN: Kids, and love and electric bills *are* everything.

(*GLORIA laughs.*)

GLORIA: Everything and nothing.

HEN: What else are you doing with someone? If that's not it –
 (*Silence.*)
GLORIA: You're having a baby. We never had children. How
 can I say – We never had children. I'm sorry.
HEN: It's fine.
GLORIA: What would I know?
 (*Silence.*)
HEN: This wasn't planned.
 (*Silence.*)
 Al, my boyfriend…he calls it a random event. He hates the
 idea of any kind of destiny. I find it hurtful. It wakes me in
 the night the thought that if this is random it could have
 been anybody's but for that one night it was me. That this
 could be someone else. He thinks I'm talking about destiny
 but I'm not. I'm talking about the fact that in meeting
 me there was nobody else. In meeting me I was the only
 mother possible for his child.
GLORIA: There's always somebody else.
 (*Silence.*)
HEN: I don't want to hear that. I'm sorry. I hear you now but
 I don't want to. I'm sorry. I'm sorry.
 (*GLORIA finally pins up the man's shirt. HEN clocks it.*)
GLORIA: There's always one that sneaks into the washing
 somehow.
 (*Silence.*)
HEN: Let's talk about…
GLORIA: Scotland.
 (*Silence.*)
HEN: Good. (*Beat.*) It should be beautiful this time of the year.

## SCENE 13

*Flat, London. MARVIN cleaning NATHAN's flat; bin bag, duster,*
*polish. An oil lamp. MARVIN flicks it on and waits. The bubble of oil*
*doesn't move. NATHAN comes through reading some papers.*

NATHAN: It needs to heat up. The oil? It won't do anything
 until it's had time to get hot, to soften.
 (*MARVIN nods. Returns to work. Dusting.*)

You okay?

MARVIN: Bin bags.

NATHAN: Top drawer.

(*MARVIN shakes out a bin bag.*)

You found them.

MARVIN: You need some more. I've put them on your list.

NATHAN: Thank you. You're finding everything okay?

MARVIN: I have a room at the hostel. Suits me fine. I can keep the same bed. If you pay in the morning you can keep the same bed.

NATHAN: And that's...

MARVIN: Suits me fine. I can keep the same bed. If you pay in the morning you keep the same bed.

NATHAN: That must be comforting.

MARVIN: That's all I need.

NATHAN: Yes.

MARVIN: You're not working...

NATHAN: Not today. (*Long beat.*) I won't get in your way.

MARVIN: That's fine. I was wondering about the ladies' things in the cupboard.

NATHAN: Yes –

MARVIN: It's just, they're taking up a lot of room, and I was wondering if you wanted me to move them down to the bigger one in the hall.

NATHAN: No.

MARVIN: (*Long beat.*) I won't bother hoovering today.

NATHAN: Thank you.

MARVIN: You need more polish as well.

NATHAN: You put it?

MARVIN: On the list.

NATHAN: Thank you.

(*Silence.*)

Marvin, you didn't always –

MARVIN: No... I've always been in cleaning of some kind but –

NATHAN: I thought not. I was thinking how's someone like him ended up –

MARVIN: I've been on a kind of holiday. Still on it really. This is my time out time. You should try it. Some time out time.

NATHAN: Yes.

MARVIN: Gives you a perspective.

NATHAN: (*Beat.*) Some things you can never get a perspective on.

MARVIN: Then you take time out until you do – (*Sniffing duster.*) Nice smell. There's nothing…there's nothing like a woman's perfume. I was just dusting some of those cupboards. It lingers.

NATHAN: There's a married man talking.

(*Silence.*)

My wife left – a while ago.

MARVIN: When you tell me that, I feel…

NATHAN: It's really very common.

MARVIN: That I understand you. That I understand what you must be going through. You didn't have…

NATHAN: Not having children makes it easier.

MARVIN: Not having children makes it possible. She wouldn't have left if you'd had children.

NATHAN: You think?

MARVIN: A child is innocent. A child is something small. Always, even when they are big, to you, a parent, they are always small. She wouldn't have left her child. That would be too much to ask you to bear.

NATHAN: Whatever.

MARVIN: It gets lonely.

(*Silence.*)

NATHAN: Opposite, you see there, the one with the blinds. There is a woman. I see her in the supermarket. She buys meals for two, enough for two people, but it's just her. I never see her with anyone. (*Looking out of window.*) Those windows out there become my friends. Those inroads into other people's lives. You must find that. As a cleaner. You are given a root in, to see the way other people live.

MARVIN: The lady who buys her meals for two buys so much because she has an elderly neighbour who can't get out herself. She divides everything she buys by two and shares it with her. I do the stairs outside her landing Tuesdays and Thursdays. The man, who you think is divorced, is not divorced. He is happily married but has chosen not to live with his wife, he spends every Sunday with her. I clean on Sundays when he is out. You see there are alternative ways of living, alternative families.

NATHAN: That's very reassuring.

MARVIN: Don't be cynical.

NATHAN: I'm not. I find that really very reassuring. People can be disappointing. Only the other week I was let down.

MARVIN: Right.

NATHAN: I had to cover for someone at work. (*Beat.*) Which was inconvenient.

MARVIN: (*Beat.*) Would you like me to do your bedroom now?

NATHAN: Yes. And in the afternoon…

MARVIN: In the afternoon?

NATHAN: I may go out.

MARVIN: And later?

NATHAN: I won't need you later.

MARVIN: I can go back to the hostel then. I don't like to be late. You can get tea between five to seven p.m.

NATHAN: That must be…

MARVIN: It's convenient. That's when I like to eat.

NATHAN: And what do you do in the evenings.

MARVIN: Sometimes I just lie on my bed and think. Or I sit at the window and listen to the different noises. Someone laughing or a shout down the corridor. And I try and work out what's happened. I set the scene in my head. The moment before, the minutes after. Or I just watch the flies zig zagging around the shade above. They move in a very definite way. Zig zag…zig zag… They leave an imaginary line, almost visible, they move so fast. Sometimes one of the other blokes, there are only men in our dormitory, sometimes one of them will go and cry out in the night and I'll go and sit at the end of whoever's bed, and share a fag, or talk, or just sometimes I just sit, even lie next

to them, hold their hand, great big men holding hands,
I never thought I'd see it, not like you think, just giving
people company, being almost tender and I stay with them
until the morning. They've normally pissed the bed or are
shouting for a drink, whatever wakes me up first – The
wet through the trousers or the great whisky breath on my
neck.

NATHAN: (*Long beat.*) Are you happy?

MARVIN: …I don't think I've ever been happier in my life.

## SCENE 14

*Restaurant, London. SQUEAL, TASH, HEN and AL are midway
through dinner. Chinese. Flock wallpaper. Shanghai Lil music.*

AL: Amputation. That's hardcore.

SQUEAL: It's just one part of the surgery I do.

AL: Wow. What do people normally have –

SQUEAL: Mainly limbs.

TASH: Please.

HEN: Please.

SQUEAL: I'm mainly casualty. Dog biscuits up the nose, that
kind of stuff –

AL: Hoovers stuck up people's arses.

HEN: Al. Stop talking like –

TASH: – a builder.

AL: (*To SQUEAL.*) She's a horror. You realise she's a horror. I
have to work around her every day.

TASH: Not every day.

AL: She doesn't get out of bed.

TASH: This is not true. I get out of bed to make you tea and
sandwiches?

HEN: You sound like an old married couple…

(*A ripple of laughter.*)

AL: You should get out more.

HEN: Why don't you go on holiday?

TASH: Maybe.

HEN: Kick start things a bit again for you.

TASH: I don't think we need to talk about this now. It's not your mission to get my life back on track.

SQUEAL: I don't mind.

HEN: Have you travelled?

SQUEAL: I did a year overseas as part of my medical training. Australia. Perth.

AL: I'd love to go to Australia. Did you know the indigenous Wallaby outnumbers the domestic dog by forty to one in the outback?

TASH: (*To SQUEAL.*) National Geographic. The Holy Grail.

HEN: I didn't know that. I didn't know you wanted to go to Australia.

AL: Yeah, you did. I'm always saying I'd love to travel.

HEN: I can't even get him to go out of London for a weekend and he's talking about Australia.

AL: That's proper travel. That's not like a weekend in Tenby. I'd like to do a lot of South East Asia as well. Malaysia, China... I've got a mate who's working on some apartments in Singapore.

SQUEAL: Singapore's fantastic. I spent a month there.

HEN: You never said this. You've never mentioned this before.

AL: I have. I've always said I'd like to travel. Maybe do India. I've always wanted to go to India.

SQUEAL: If you're doing India, you've got to head south. Sri Lanka.

AL: Yeah.

SQUEAL: It's an amazing country. I mean really amazing. I mean I'm not talking about all the tourism and the sleazy end of it but if you really spend some time there. It's Buddhist and yet there's a lot of Catholicism so you've got these two faiths side by side. You can be driving down the road and on one side you've got these fantastic Buddhist Temples, I mean really ornate and yet go in them and it's so humble, so peaceful. I mean I'm not religious, but there you start to believe in something beyond this, something linking us all then on the other side you've got all hell and damnation and then you start looking at the Buddhist temples again and you realise it's all just the same thing. They've got devils and demons and crocodiles eating elephants and its just everyone trying to believe in something beyond themselves. Know what I mean?

AL: Yeah. Yeah. And somewhere, I don't know where it is, there's this, there's this waterfall that falls down into this inland pool that's so deep that no one has ever actually got to the bottom and you can go there and stay days because all around the edges are these tiny caves and you build fires and sleep by the water at night and in the day you can do this trek to the top of the waterfall and people do these river jumps and they say if you do touch the bottom you've been touched by the hand of God and that if you survive it – you grow a third leg that turns into a fin over night.

(*AL starts laughing.*)

TASH: Funny. Very funny. Did anyone get that down?

AL: Sorry…mate… Sorry.

TASH: (*To AL.*) You're an arse.

SQUEAL: You're alright.

HEN: It sounds beautiful. It sounds amazing.

SQUEAL: It is.

HEN: (*Beat.*) We should go then.

SQUEAL: I've got some books on it if you want to have a look.

AL: It might be a bit hard with the baby.

TASH: You can do anything with a baby. I bet there were people out there with babies. Life goes on with a baby.

AL: It would with you, yeah. But then life goes on with whatever, doesn't it Tash? No job, you just get another, no bloke just pick up another fuck for the night.

HEN: Al –

AL: You do know she's incapable of sustaining anything she won't be able to rip down and replaster next week.

TASH: I'm not listening.

AL: When was the last time anyone said they'd loved you, Tash?

TASH: What's this turnaround?

AL: When?

TASH: You'll be the first to know.

AL: Not yet then. Point proven. Incapable.

TASH: That really is straight to the nuts even for you.

AL: It's what people say to each other.

HEN: Give it a rest, Al.

AL: It's what people feel for each other –

(*Silence.*)

When?

(*Silence.*)

When?

(*Silence.*)

SQUEAL: I love her.

(*Silence.*)

TASH: You hardly know me.

SQUEAL: I wasn't saying marrry me.

TASH: Don't give me the sympathy vote.

HEN: Tash –

TASH: You love me. Is that what you think I need? You think that does the trick? I'm not a charity.

SQUEAL: I didn't do that for a good cause.

TASH: Why did you then?

(*Silence.*)

I wasn't incarcerated and I wasn't abused. I have very nice parents and a brother with three kids. He's normal, too normal some might say. I have a healthy appetite, I don't get into abusive relationships, I don't get into relationships, I wasn't bullied and I had a fantastic time at college, career's a bit shaky but fuck it I've still got my own teeth, so the last thing I need –

SQUEAL: Forget it.

TASH: You're the one who's embarrassed yourself.

(*Silence. TASH exits. SQUEAL, AL and HEN sit in silence.*)

HEN: (*Beat.*) You never said you wanted to travel.

AL: Someone was just talking about it at work.

HEN: Someone?

(*Silence. HEN scrapes her chair back and exits. AL and SQUEAL sit in silence until –*)

SQUEAL: Shall I get the bill?

# SCENE 15

*Flat, London. Morning. NATHAN is making breakfast. Coffee, bagels, cream cheese. Sound of a shower turning off. NATHAN waits until – TASH comes through in a towel.*

NATHAN: You found –
TASH: Yeah.
(*NATHAN nods, pours TASH a cup of coffee. TASH picks up a shoe.*)
One more to go.
NATHAN: I've got bagels.
TASH: (*Beat.*) Great.
(*TASH exits. NATHAN starts to toast bagels, read the paper, flick around with the radio until – TASH comes back through, now half dressed, pulling on her shirt, the same clothes from the night before. NATHAN slides her over a cup of coffee.*)
Thanks. I'm sorry… I'm sorry I didn't show last week.
NATHAN: I had to cover –
TASH: Yeah.
NATHAN: I had to cover for you.
TASH: Yeah. I'm sorry.
NATHAN: It's probably, it's probably a sackable offence.
(*TASH laughs. NATHAN laughs. NATHAN goes to talk to her. TASH moves away.*)
TASH: Nice coffee.
NATHAN: Yeah.
TASH: Good.
NATHAN: Bagel.
TASH: Great.
(*TASH doesn't touch her breakfast.*)
I don't normally eat breakfast.
NATHAN: Right. Okay. Don't worry. Would you like cereal?
TASH: No, coffee's great.
(*Silence. TASH drinks, unsure what to do next.*)
I used some of your shampoo and a toothbrush as well.
NATHAN: Mia casa your casa.
(*Silence.*)
TASH: I might get a move on then.

NATHAN: Now.

TASH: Yeah.

NATHAN: I thought we could –

TASH: No. Sorry.

NATHAN: It's just last night –

TASH: I didn't want to go home.

NATHAN: I thought we could spend the day together.

TASH: Please. I know where this is going – I'm sorry but
that's not the way it works. Why don't people get that? I
don't know why you like me. Is it because I'm here? You
seem like a very nice guy. A very nice lonely guy.

NATHAN: No.

TASH: Who thinks that I'm the answer. But I'm not...

(*Silence.*)

NATHAN: Right.

(*Silence.*)

TASH: I was lonely. I was lonely too last night.

(*Silence.*)

You live close.

NATHAN: Of course. Sure. Of course.

TASH: I feel a shit now.

NATHAN: Don't –

(*Silence.*)

Why should you feel bad? We both got what we want.

TASH: Not exactly.

NATHAN: So shall we say Monday?

TASH: You serious?

NATHAN: You want a job don't you?

(*Silence. TASH nods.*)

TASH: I used the hairbrush as well. There were a lot of
blonde hairs and I'm dark so if she sees, whoever she is,
can you apologise –

(*Silence.*)

I wasn't really looking for anything more than –

NATHAN: Someone to lie with.

TASH: Yeah. (*Beat.*) So it didn't matter.

(*Silence.*)

Everyone has that problem once in a while.

NATHAN: Not me. I bring girls back all the time.

TASH: Yeah.

NATHAN: Yeah. So really it made a change.

TASH: I should go.

NATHAN: Yeah.

(*TASH wavers at the door. Silence.*)

TASH: I was out for supper last night. With a friend, my best friend and her boyfriend and we got into this sort of fight and I was with another friend and we were coming home and suddenly I just couldn't be on my own. I couldn't think where else to go.

NATHAN: (*Beat.*) Sure.

(*TASH nods.*)

TASH: See you Monday.

(*TASH makes to go.*)

NATHAN: Looking forward to it. (*Beat.*) You know you really are quite a cunt.

(*TASH hesitates, exits. NATHAN sits on his own. He stares down at the second cup of coffee and bagel. He suddenly gets up, scoops up plates, bagel, cup in one move and shoves it in the sink.*)

## SCENE 16

*Bed and Breakfast, Scotland. GLORIA is standing brushing her teeth. She is talking to herself.*

GLORIA: Not today. Please not today. Yesterday, when I needed you, where were you? Not today. I was walking and I was looking for you everywhere. Do you know how many pubs there are? Sitting on my own in a pub, hoping – Marvin? And I had this thought, it crossed my mind, it was more a feeling, a very strong sensation, that when you're in my mind, every moment that I'm thinking of you, every blinding, boring moment, that I'm carrying you close to me, talking to you, wanting you…you want no one. Not me. No one. You need no one. I feel sick. I want to vomit. I want to –

(*GLORIA looks at herself in the mirror, as she waits in expectation of some kind of response. She breathes heavy against the mirror.*)
Skye.
(*The squawk of gulls outside, making her turn and look out for a moment. She returns to cleaning her teeth, finishes, picks up a towel, her costume, contemplates with terror.*)
Come back. Come back. I don't know how much longer –
(*The lap of sea water.*)

## SCENE 17

*Bar, London. TASH and HEN sitting perched, drinking. Noise all around.*

TASH: Forget it.

HEN: No, it was horrible of him.

TASH: I've know him too long. I've known you both too long. It was fine.

HEN: I felt terrible.

TASH: Friends, good friends have those kind of…scuffles.

HEN: He's cooking tonight.

TASH: He said. I saw the…

HEN: Curry. He always cooks curry.

TASH: And you always hate it. Why don't you say to him?

HEN: Too late. Should have done it years ago but now… I've been eating it and telling him I love it. We've bonded over that curry. We've made babies over that curry. (*Beat.*) You saw Al today –

TASH: (*Beat.*) He's almost finished the bathroom.

HEN: Well when he's finished with yours ask if he can knock ours on the head, eh? I don't know if we're ever going to get into that house.

TASH: You can have him back anytime you want.

HEN: Has it made it difficult?

TASH: It's fine. We both ignored it… It was ignored the next day. (*Beat.*) He had a point.

HEN: He cares about you. (*Beat.*) He cares about me, therefore he cares about you. (*Beat.*) He does.

129

TASH: Are you feeling – ?

HEN: Great... Fat... Fat and ugly...

TASH: No...

HEN: Yes.

TASH: This is when you say... 'He doesn't want to sleep with me anymore.'

HEN: (*Beat.*) He doesn't want to sleep with me anymore.
(*Beat.*) Not.
(*A ripple of laughter.*)
Have you seen –

TASH: This bar is really noisy.

HEN: Deflection.

TASH: Overturned. I don't want to talk about –

HEN: I didn't say anything.

TASH: I don't want to talk about him. Do you need some kind of reassurance? Am I some kind of loose cannon like you want to partner me up?

HEN: It's okay... It's okay...

TASH: Why do you always say that? 'It's okay...it's okay...'

HEN: Sorry...

TASH: Stop it will you...

HEN: What?

TASH: Please, fight back a bit Hen –

HEN: This is not important enough. We've had a good evening. Why are you spoiling it now? You've had a bad day? I'm sorry if you've had a bad day.

TASH: I've not had a bad day... Stop accommodating me...

HEN: What have I done? I don't get it... This is what I do... I listen... You talk...

TASH: I know.

HEN: Is there something you're not telling me?

TASH: No...

HEN: Tash...

TASH: Just back off Hen. Your life's okay, alright?

HEN: I never said it wasn't. *I* never said it wasn't. Is Al sleeping with someone?

TASH: You're so fucking dramatic.

HEN: I'd rather know.

TASH: I was talking about me –

HEN: Is that why you brought me here?

TASH: No. Hen? (*Long beat.*) No... He loves you.

HEN: How do you know?

TASH: He does. Where's all this come from?

    (*Silence.*)

    He does.

    (*Silence.*)

HEN: Liar.

    (*HEN orders another drink.*)


## SCENE 18

*Flat, London. MARVIN entering the flat, pausing on seeing –*

NATHAN: (*Calling out.*) Marvin –

    (*A row of woman's clothes, dresses etc., hanging up, in bags as
    if ready to be thrown out as NATHAN comes through carrying
    more dresses on hangers.*)

    If there's anything you would like take it.

    (*NATHAN exits. MARVIN goes over and touches the dresses
    as NATHAN comes through carrying boxes of shoes.*)

    Obviously that's not your colour but I thought maybe
    people at the hostel.

MARVIN: It's all men.

NATHAN: (*Beat.*) There's some good coats.

    (*NATHAN exits. MARVIN opens one of the boxes, takes out
    a shoe as NATHAN comes back through, two big bin bags in
    hand.*)

    I think it's a waste leaving them kicking around in the back
    of a cupboard when somebody could be getting pleasure
    out of them.

MARVIN: Right.

NATHAN: I could drive you to the charity shops if you don't
    want them.

MARVIN: That might be an idea.

NATHAN: We could pick up some supper after.

MARVIN: I have to be back at the hostel.

NATHAN: Let your hair down for a night, Marvin. When was
    the last time you went to a restaurant?

MARVIN: I go to Starbucks most days.

NATHAN: I want to take you out.

(*NATHAN exits.*)

MARVIN: (*Calling out.*) Oxfam is the nearest.

(*As NATHAN comes back through with the last bag.*)

NATHAN: Whatever.

(*Clocking MARVIN watching him.*)

You're always telling me to clear out that cupboard.

(*MARVIN nods, he looks at the shoe in his hand.*)

MARVIN: These are beautiful.

NATHAN: They've already dated. They're fashionable so I suppose they date quicker.

MARVIN: They're still beautiful.

(*MARVIN looks at the tiny straps of the shoe.*)

You forget how thin a woman's ankle is.

NATHAN: Yes.

(*MARVIN nods, carefully puts the shoe back.*)

MARVIN: My wife liked –

(*Silence.*)

I'll clean out that room then.

(*NATHAN nods. MARVIN makes to go, pulling off his coat.*)

NATHAN: And after we'll go out and eat.

MARVIN: I have to be back at the hostel before eight.

NATHAN: They don't lock you in. You can come and go, surely.

MARVIN: I like the routine.

NATHAN: For one night –

(*Silence.*)

MARVIN: I'll say no. But thank you.

(*Silence. MARVIN makes to go.*)

NATHAN: Marvin, I want you to come out to supper tonight. You've been a very good friend to me these last few weeks. Steak. You like steak I bet.

MARVIN: I don't eat meat much now.

NATHAN: Well tonight –

MARVIN: I don't really like going out. I've found a life that suits me. I don't mean to be rude, Nathan. You're a good boy but –

NATHAN: Say yes. Please say fucking yes Marvin. Say yes.

MARVIN: I'm your cleaner.

NATHAN: You're saying no.

MARVIN: I prefer to – I prefer just to work if you don't mind.

NATHAN: I'll pay you. How much do you cost for a night? Just for the company.

MARVIN: You must have friends. A man like you must have –

NATHAN: I want someone I don't know. I want a friend I don't know. Tell me about yourself Marvin. Your wife?

MARVIN: I'll clean the back room.

NATHAN: Twenty – twenty-five, I'll give you twenty-five quid. (*Beat.*) We could go to the cashpoint.

(*NATHAN starts trying to shove money into MARVIN's hand. MARVIN stands embarrassed.*)

MARVIN: Please –

NATHAN: I just want someone to have a fucking pizza with –

(*Silence.*)

It was just an idea.

MARVIN: A nice idea.

(*Silence.*)

Why don't you get one of your lady friends to take you out?

(*Silence.*)

I wouldn't be able to pay.

(*NATHAN shrugs.*)

Nathan, have you thought of going to talk to someone?

(*NATHAN half laughs to himself.*)

I'll clean the bathroom while I'm at it.

(*NATHAN nods.*)

NATHAN: I don't understand you. I don't understand people.

(*Silence.*)

I'll get changed then. I'm starving.

(*NATHAN exits. MARVIN is left standing looking at all the clothes. He goes to touch them and them stops himself.*)

# SCENE 19

*Bedroom, London. HEN and AL are lying in bed.*

HEN: We don't do this –

AL: No.

HEN: We don't do this enough. Like being on holiday.

AL: A one hour holiday.

HEN: A lunch hour holiday. (*Sudden start.*) Did you feel it move?

AL: What?

HEN: It moved. More than a nudge, a real kick.

AL: I felt nothing.

HEN: Wait. (*Long wait.*) Feel?

AL: No, nothing.

HEN: Never mind.

AL: Footballer. It's definitely going to be a footballer.

HEN: Yes. (*Long beat.*) Have you talked to Tash yet?

AL: No.

HEN: You ought to say sorry.

AL: No.

HEN: It was cruel what you said.

AL: It was true.

HEN: She hasn't rung all week.

AL: Enjoy the peace.

HEN: Blokes never get, they never get girlfriends.

AL: I have mates.

HEN: Yeah but not like girlfriends. (*Beat.*) This is nice.

AL: Uh huh.

HEN: It's just…

AL: Something on your mind…

HEN: Someone finishing my sentences before I ever get to the end of them. Sorry. Sorry.

AL: ( *Jumping up.*) Jesus… That was a Beckham punch. I felt it…

HEN: Did you?

AL: Right in the face. Really big boot right in the chops.

HEN: See. That's what I'm living with. That's what I'm waking up with.

AL: Uh huh...

HEN: To find you're not home... (*Long silence.*) Where were you Thursday night?

AL: Home.

HEN: No, you weren't. I woke up. I woke up at three and you weren't even back.

AL: It was eleven. You'd just gone to sleep. I promise you.

HEN: And I felt a kick in my stomach and I opened my eyes thinking it was you but you weren't home. So I waited up and when you did creep in at 4.30... I'd closed my eyes and pretended I was asleep, with it still kicking me, with me wanting to scream out and you just lay there with your eyes open, not moving...

AL: No...

HEN: And your face smelt. You hadn't even bothered to wash your face.

AL: Hen... This is mad...

HEN: Tell me then different. Tell me different...

AL: I don't know what you're talking about.

HEN: I do... I do...

## SCENE 20

*Office, London. GLORIA sits tapping details into a computer. NATHAN sits opposite. He shifts in his chair, as if short of time.*

GLORIA: A natural blonde. That's very rare now.

NATHAN: I thought she was but after... When she'd gone, I discovered the hair bleach... She dyed it, and yet she'd always told me that it was her own natural colour.

GLORIA: A white lie. Husbands and wives need little white lies.

NATHAN: She was a very honest person. She was a very straight person.

GLORIA: It's a nice name.

NATHAN: It still has a kind of magic for me. I find it disturbing when I meet other people who have the same name. A lot of faces. (*Pointing.*) On the walls. A lot of people missing.

GLORIA: Yes. But they are found. Many of them, the majority of them are eventually traced. Do you have a job?

NATHAN: Yes... I'm freelance now... I work when I feel like it.

GLORIA: Who for?

NATHAN: Myself... People. I have been recording people. On film. Notating them down. Their habits.

GLORIA: For?

NATHAN: Clients.

GLORIA: You're an academic.

NATHAN: Yes... It's a kind of research...

GLORIA: Gloria.

NATHAN: Gloria. Do you get paid for this?

GLORIA: No... (*Beat.*) My husband has been gone now... 14 months and 12 days...

NATHAN: You count the days.

GLORIA: Without hesitation. It just happens.

NATHAN: It's the waiting...

GLORIA: We have to find a way of living in the waiting.

NATHAN: But if they don't come back.

GLORIA: Then your time hasn't been wasted. You should try a hobby.

NATHAN: I don't think so. I don't really have the time...

GLORIA: You have the whole of your life.

NATHAN: What if the person was your life? What if that one person was everything?

GLORIA: No one person is everything.

NATHAN: You were obviously married a long time. I don't mean to be rude. You have something to hold onto. We weren't married very long. I worry I'm forgetting her. I don't want to move on.

GLORIA: That's your choice.

NATHAN: You're very hard.

GLORIA: No.

NATHAN: Yes you are. You're hard.

GLORIA: I'm softer than I've ever been. I'm more open than I've ever been. I walk down the street and I notice people. Their pain. Their discomfort. Their happiness. I drink it in. I have my eyes open. I swim. Every day I swim. Back and forth. A routine. A boring routine that becomes so familiar I grow almost fond of it. I imagine myself swimming far out and not coming back. But how far away is forever? How far away before that place becomes my life? So I stay. In my pain, in my vulnerability, in my isolation and in this nakedness I feel reborn. Like a baby. I am standing in the world like a dripping baby. More open than I have ever been. He has made me more open than I have ever been.

NATHAN: You're not grateful? You're grateful that he left you?

GLORIA: I live with a kind of understanding.

NATHAN: Until he comes back? (*Long beat.*) What if he never comes back?

GLORIA: I live with that.

NATHAN: I thought you were meant to give people hope. I thought you were meant to show me a way to find my wife.

GLORIA: How long has she been gone...

NATHAN: Nathan.

GLORIA: Nathan.

NATHAN: 2 years, 4 months. I don't do days.

GLORIA: That's a long time. Nathan...

NATHAN: (*Long beat.*) They found her with a belt around her neck. It always throws people. She's a banker. Was a... She fucks up on some shares. I tell her she won't lose her job. She does. I tell her I love her. I tell her... She mustn't have loved me. Professional suicide. I urinate on her boss's desk a week later. Piss all over the trading room floor. It seems a riot at the time. I lose my job. With sympathy and condolences. I come home and I sit down and I realise I don't like any of the furniture. I sleep around. It makes me feel liberated. I'm envied by all my mates. The best of both worlds. A taste of both sides of the coin. Married and single. 'You lucky cunt!' I miss my wife? 'No.' (*Long beat.*) I realise that I can't remember her face yet I find her features everywhere. Fixing her eyes with the lips of others. My cleaner tells me I am sick. I get her pissed and fuck her. She doesn't speak much English but I think we don't enjoy it. She leaves. I have a new one, a man working for me now. I get myself a new job. (*Beat.*) I try to work out

my wife's thoughts. Retrace her steps. She comes home.
Has a sandwich. Doesn't even wash up after herself. She's
lazy like that. Walks to the bathroom. Takes off her clothes,
turns on the shower...

GLORIA: Your wife is dead?

NATHAN: She's missing, she's very much missing in my life.

GLORIA: (*Long beat.*) Is listening enough?

NATHAN: I don't know... I don't know if it helps at all.

(*GLORIA looks up from her work. NATHAN is staring out
and beyond her. The lap of water building into a shower.*)

## SCENE 21

*Bar, London. TASH running in to meet HEN who sits at the bar,
drinking a glass of red wine. It is raining outside. It's very quiet.*

TASH: Did you not hear me? I was shouting you half way
down the street. You could have an accident driving like
that. I was waving my knickers off. Did you not see me?
Hen...

HEN: I saw.

TASH: I thought you worked late on Thursday. If you saw
me you could have given me a lift. I'm wet now. I'm really
wet.

HEN: I gave in my notice.

TASH: That thing's on the downward slope, I should hope so.
(*Looking out for barman.*) Could I?

HEN: I had to wait...

TASH: Never mind...okay... So your time is now your own.

HEN: Yeah.

TASH: That's good. That's great. This is a treat.

HEN: You always...

TASH: Used to like this bar. Do not like this bar anymore. Do
not like the lack of *service*.

HEN: Don't make a fuss.

TASH: I'm not making a fuss. At least it's quiet. I thought
you'd like that.

HEN: Have you been drinking?

TASH: Celebrating. The flat. It's finished, I finished the back bedroom last night. Al was well miffed.

HEN: Uh huh?

TASH: He's an arse. He's charged me a fortune.

HEN: You love me.

TASH: I love you, therefore I negotiate around him but still...

HEN: I know.

TASH: I hope you do by now because I wouldn't last another week having him in my house. He better have done me a cheap deal.

HEN: I know about you and him.

TASH: Sorry?

HEN: I know where he is on Thursday night. I know what he gets up to. (*Beat.*) I know you're sleeping with him.

TASH: Right. (*Long beat.*) And you're going to leave him?

HEN: You weren't meant to take my husband.

TASH: Partner.

HEN: Did you do this on purpose? Did you want to hurt me? Are you very unhappy, Tash? Are you so unhappy that you couldn't...? Was it so awful to see me settled? What's in you that you have to destroy everything?

TASH: That's the way you see it.

HEN: Fact.

TASH: That's the way you see it.

HEN: I don't know what to do now. What am I meant to do now? Who am I meant to go to now?

TASH: You'll make yourself...

HEN: I have this thing to shit out. I have this thing to love and look after.

TASH: Why don't we go to mine?

HEN: And I try and understand that. I try and sympathise with you. Tash, I care if you're unhappy, but it is not my fault that you can't find a man of your own. Some people find love difficult. So I've tried to be there for you and you do something like this.

TASH: He told you?

HEN: I smelt you on him.

TASH: He told you?

HEN: He came home smelling of you.

TASH: Did he say?

HEN: He's being so sweet. So nice. So desperate. Last night he cried. He said *please don't leave me.* And I realise what you do. You go in and you scorch the surface of anyone else's relationship. I'm so angry with you. I don't know what to do. I want to love you, Tash. I want to love you, but you make it hard. Perhaps you should talk to someone. You should go and see someone and talk to them, because I can't love you anymore. This baby needs me now. Al needs me now. I've tried with you. (*Beat.*) I can't trust you anymore.

TASH: But you forgive him.

HEN: No, I don't forgive him. But this is longer than a friendship. We have to be bigger than this. If you'd just come and told me how you felt, Tash. I would have understood. If you just told me you were so jealous.

TASH: He told you?

HEN: I smelt you.

TASH: He told you.

HEN: *Please don't leave me.*

TASH: She's twenty-two. The foreman's daughter. I don't know her name.

HEN: I've loved you. I've cared about you. I've shared everything with you.

TASH: He fucks her over the photocopier. They're careless with the prints.

HEN: He said you'd say this.

TASH: The girl thinks she's in love with him. I found them in his bag.

HEN: Why are you doing this?

TASH: His foreman has warned Al he'll sack him if he finds him doing it again.

HEN: He said, you would...

TASH: Listen to me... I agreed he should work at mine to get him away from the site.

HEN: I promised him, I wouldn't leave him.

TASH: You can do it.

HEN: I promised him.

TASH: I didn't want to tell you.

HEN: He said...

TASH: I've never...

HEN: It's easier... (*Beat.*) Somehow it's easier if it is you...

TASH: No...

HEN: If it could have just been anybody...just anybody...
then who's to say it's love with me? (*Beat.*) I smelt you on
him.

TASH: No...

HEN: I smelt you on him.

TASH: Hen.

HEN: No.

TASH: My betrayal's easier than his? (*Long beat.*) There's
nowhere to go then.

(*HEN and TASH look at one another. HEN slides over her
drink. TASH knocks it back.*)

## SCENE 22

*Loft, London. NATHAN is undressing as if getting ready for a shower.
He drapes his shirt over the rail above. The sound of the shower
throughout.*

NATHAN: They fired her the day the market slumped. She
never stood a chance. They're going bust. She calls me in
high agitation. 'I've fucked them up the wall.' 'I'm busy,
sweetheart. Can't we talk later?' (*Beat.*) Ask me how she
looked that day and I struggle to remember her face.
Doesn't that suck? Don't forget to look at your lover, don't
forget to breathe her in, taste her, know her... She took a
belt... Like this one... She hooked it over the shower head.
(*The sound of the hoover being turned off.*)
Why didn't the bastard break? She washed herself. Ready
and then – (*Slipping the belt off around his waist.*) For a tiny
moment I can feel her. Warm against my skin – (*Slipping
the belt around his neck.*) I'm sorry. (*Beat.*) I get so lonely.
(*MARVIN enters as NATHAN swings from the rail above.
MARVIN does not move for a moment until he struggles to get*

*him down. He slips on the floor with him. He tries to revive*
*him. He slowly realises that he is already dead.*
*A build of a baby's wail.)*

# SCENE 23

*Flat, London. HEN packing up a tea chest of china. AL enters. He's*
*dressed down, shorts, trainers, a younger look.*

AL: I didn't see your car...

HEN: Walked.

AL: I could help you with this.

HEN: No, I'm fine... (*Beat.*) You've let this place –

AL: I was going to tidy up.

HEN: Really get a mess.

    (*HEN goes to pick up an empty tea chest.*)

AL: Let me.

HEN: No.

AL: (*Long beat.*) He's sleeping?

HEN: Right through. This easy I'll have another this time next
    year.

AL: Your mum?

HEN: Taking me in until –

AL: The house'll –

HEN: – never be finished.

AL: – not for a while yet. I never said –

HEN: – anything that wasn't true.

AL: – sorry.

HEN: No.

AL: Sorry.

HEN: (*Long beat.*) Not accepted...

AL: Hen...

HEN: There are random moments and moments of decision.
    You said that...

AL: I didn't mean...

HEN: Some of the biggest moments in my life have been
    founded on those two principles.

AL: Hen, if I could...

HEN: No... No... Yours was a moment of decision. (*Eyeing him.*) You going on –

AL: Holiday.

HEN: Yeah.

AL: Going to India.

HEN: Yeah. (*Beat.*) With? She's young enough to be your –

AL: It's only a –

(*AL starts to help HEN pack up. They work in silence.*)

What am I doing, Hen?

HEN: I don't know.

(*AL reaches out for HEN's hand. She holds it.*)

AL: Please.

HEN: No. You can't come back. You can't.

## SCENE 24

*Flat, London. Late night. TASH staggers in. She's pissed. She slams down keys and her bag and goes over to the fridge. She opens it. It casts its light, sending its hum around the room. She contemplates it.*

TASH: And then what?

(*SQUEAL sits in the half light.*)

SQUEAL: There are pockets of water, just spinning in space, small oceans of water which are lifeless, dead, or as we know it at the moment but which may well have the breadth and depth of some of our own larger seas.

TASH: But what glues them together? What holds them?

SQUEAL: Gravity.

TASH: Like a skin.

SQUEAL: A skin of gravity which envelopes them and changes form in motion.

TASH: Like amoeba.

SQUEAL: Like an amoeba.

TASH: Or a puddle.

SQUEAL: Not a puddle. But they can break up.

TASH: Like a worm.

SQUEAL: I'll go with a worm. (*Beat.*) You drink too much.

TASH: I don't drink enough.

SQUEAL: I'd like to see you. I'd like to talk to you. In the daytime. Not in the dark.

TASH: You wouldn't cope.

SQUEAL: You think?

(*TASH holds his stare, lets this moment hang between them.*)

TASH: Tell me the fighter pilot story.

SQUEAL: You've heard it.

TASH: Tell me it again.

SQUEAL: I'm useless at everything, except physics. I am the maestro of physics. I do all the tests. I'm top of it all. But I can't tell the difference between green and red. Stop or go. I fail.

(*TASH laughs to herself, finishing off her cornflakes, laughing to herself, letting it die between them.*)

It would be good to get further than this story you know. I'd like us to try and get beyond.

TASH: This is it.

SQUEAL: I don't believe that. I really truly don't believe that.

TASH: I wake up in the night and I'm almost breathless. Like I'm holding the exhale. Like to breathe out fully will kill me, shatter me, let me feel the full breadth of my empty bed. Just me and nothing. My thoughts. And sometimes the feeling is so desperate. And the only thing that gets me to sleep is to touch myself. Run my fingers over myself, bring myself to some kind of inner connection, do something that creates an involuntary sensation, shuddering through me, like the ghost of someone, the spirit of someone fucking me. It's not that I think that people always leave. I just don't contemplate they'll stay. (*Long beat.*) It's...painful.

(*SQUEAL leans forward in his chair, almost touching her. TASH sits motionless, suddenly frozen, trying to focus on his face.*)

TASH: (*Long beat.*) I've pissed myself.

SQUEAL: Lucky I'm here then.

# SCENE 25

*SQUEAL running, swimming towel in hand as if late for GLORIA.*

SQUEAL: I'm sorry.

GLORIA: Keep your hair on. It's fine.

SQUEAL: I can't actually stay today.

GLORIA: Oh –

SQUEAL: It's just –

GLORIA: You're meeting someone? You're meeting someone.

SQUEAL: Yes.

GLORIA: Don't be miserable about it. It's good news isn't it?

   (*Silence.*)

   I might just do a few laps.

SQUEAL: This doesn't mean –

GLORIA: What? You're dumping me? Got you worried. It's a
   good thing.

SQUEAL: It might just be a meeting.

GLORIA: You might be –

SQUEAL: I'm not.

GLORIA: Yeah, I'm going to do a few laps today.

SQUEAL: Gloria –

GLORIA: Look at you. For a start, you better get your hair
   cut. I've been meaning to tell you for some time. Smarten
   up a bit for – Whoever.

   (*SQUEAL shrugs, makes to go.*)

SQUEAL: From the back. The way your hair goes. The way
   the colour goes. First time I met you, you reminded me of
   my –

GLORIA: Cheeky bugger. (*Suddenly.*) I wish I had. Would
   have drowned you at birth. My luck.

SQUEAL: Yeah right.

GLORIA: Go on. She'll be waiting. I don't mean to be
   ungrateful.

   (*SQUEAL looks away.*)

SQUEAL: Gloria, keep your thumbs with your fingers. It'll
   stop you splashing so much.

   (*SQUEAL looks back. GLORIA has already gone, swimming
   away.*)

# SCENE 26

*Pool, London. TASH sitting reading her book, waiting for someone – MARVIN dressed in black. He has clearly been at a funeral. He sits on the bench next to TASH.*

MARVIN: Good book?

    (*TASH nods. Continues reading.*)

    Long time since I read a good book.

    (*TASH nods. Shifts slightly in her seat. Ignores him.*)

    Talk to me. (*Beat.*) I've just watched them bury a man.

    (*Beat.*) Talk to me.

TASH: I'm sorry…

MARVIN: Say whatever you want. Say whatever comes into your head. Just say something.

TASH: (*Long beat.*) Yes… It's a good book.

MARVIN: Adventure?

TASH: No… Sort of… A love story. Not a romantic love story… It's a tragedy yet it also has hope. I haven't finished it yet.

MARVIN: Of course.

TASH: Did you…

MARVIN: No. I hardly knew him.

TASH: Right. I hate funerals. It's alright if they have a lot to drink. I've been to a wake before. You can't fail to have a good time at a wake.

MARVIN: He was young. He was a young man.

TASH: That's awful.

MARVIN: Yes.

TASH: How did he…

MARVIN: He died because he wasn't loved, because he thought he wasn't loved.

TASH: I see. I'm sorry…

MARVIN: I come here most days.

TASH: You must be very…

MARVIN: Yes… Shaken… Yes… I'm very shaken, but I understand it you see. You think you are not loved or maybe you have stopped being able to feel that you are so you withdraw. And the hardest place to be is with people

but not with people. Alone in a crowded room. And
sometimes it is your fault because you don't feel anything
so you have to go away in order to decide if you want to
come back. And when you don't. When what you have
been looking for finds you, then you hope that they will
forgive you. You hope they won't feel the pain that boy
felt, you hope they'll understand that you do still think of
them...

TASH: I'm sure they will.

MARVIN: Becaue you have to live with the not being sure.
You have to...

TASH: I'm very sorry for your loss.

(*MARVIN nods. TASH gets up to go.*)

MARVIN: It's a nice park. It has a view of the pool.

TASH: Yes, I guess it does.

(*TASH gets up to go. She leaves her book. MARVIN picks it
up and starts to read it. TASH comes back for it. He hands it
to her.*)

MARVIN: I won't be staying long anyway.

(*TASH takes the book, smiles and exits. MARVIN stands up.
His gaze follows someone very slowly in the distance. A gentle
rhythm, barely visible back and forth.*)

(*Silent.*) Gloria –

(*He turns and exits. The lap of water.*)

# SCENE 27

*Pool, London. GLORIA is standing in her swimming costume and
swimming cap, dripping wet.*

GLORIA: And the sea is icy but I'm not scared. I wade in
quickly. It is dark and I can see the shadows of clouds
moving above. The water moves around me. It's cold and
yet with every stroke I feel myself getting warmer. Like
being held, suspended, above it all. And soon I can't see
where I have come from or how far I have gone. Just me
in the water in the middle of the sea, looking up at the
dark sky above. And I think how easy it would be just to

let go, just to keep swimming, until I am too exhausted and my legs and arms won't hold me. I could just let the sea take me, just wash me away, when I look up and there are a pair of eyes staring back at me. A seal, staring at me, circling me. And I feel no fear, no cold just utterly and absolutely not alone. Five minutes, ten minutes no more and it's gone. And without me even doing anything I'm suddenly turning and swimming back, not looking behind me, just swimming back to the bay, swimming back to land. Just a woman, too fat for her costume, dripping wet and cold, standing on a piece of Skye. Glad she didn't drown. Glad she didn't…

(*GLORIA turns slowly to look behind her, as if checking for someone for a moment. Nothing. She starts to dry herself, rubbing harder as the lights go down.*)

*The End.*

# Note

In addition to the above play, short snapshot scenes were added during scene changes. These are an option and are to be placed at the discretion of the production.

## INSERT 1

*TASH runs back, hurrying after SQUEAL.*

TASH: 8806 2424.
(*SQUEAL stops, silently amazed.*)
I changed my mind.
(*TASH turns and runs off. SQUEAL stands, silently bemused in the rain, trying to remember a telephone number.*)
SQUEAL: Has anyone got a pen?

## INSERT 2

*NATHAN and MARVIN are bent peering over the fridge.*

NATHAN: Fruit to the left. Dairy to the right. If you could clean it Monday, Wednesday and Friday, after you've done the surfaces and wiped through.
MARVIN: Right.
NATHAN: Hoovering thereafter.
MARVIN: Okay.
NATHAN: Good. Good.
(*They sit.*)
MARVIN: Nice fridge.
NATHAN: Thank you. I don't like my dairy and fruit too close.

Printed in the USA
CPSIA information can be obtained
at www.ICGtesting.com
LVHW020841171024
794056LV00002B/326